FLIGHT PERFORMANCE & PL

CW01477044

Dr. Stuart E. Smith

STUDY GUIDE SERIES for EASA examinations

British Library Cataloguing in Publication Data.
A catalogue record for this book is pending from the British Library.

First published in the United Kingdom by Cranfield Aviation Training School Limited. 2002

Further volumes in this series are:
Aircraft General Knowledge: Airframes / Systems / Powerplant / Electrics / Emergency Equipment
Air Law
General Navigation
Human Performance
Instruments
Mass & Balance
Meteorology
Operational Procedures
Performance
Principles of Flight
Radio Navigation
VFR & IFR Communications

Series editor: Dr. Stuart E. Smith

CRANFIELD AVIATION TRAINING SCHOOL LTD. PART-FCL ATO N° 276
CATS INNOVATION CENTRE, LUTON, Bedfordshire LU2 8DL U.K.   www.catsaviation.com

Flight Planning & Monitoring

CRANFIELD AVIATION TRAINING SCHOOL LTD. PART-FCL ATO N° 276
CATS INNOVATION CENTRE, LUTON, Bedfordshire LU2 8DL U.K.

www.catsaviation.com

i

Flight Planning & Monitoring

CHAPTER 1
Planning General

AIRLINE TRANSPORT PILOTS LICENCE
(030 00 00 00 - FLIGHT PERFORMANCE AND PLANNING)
033 00 00 00 FLIGHT PLANNING AND FLIGHT MONITORING
033 01 00 00 FLIGHT PLANS FOR CROSS-COUNTRY FLIGHTS FOR VFR FLIGHTS
033 01 01 00 Completing a navigation plan
033 01 01 01 Selection of routes, speeds, heights (altitudes) and alternate airfield
-Select a route and altitude taking the following criteria into account:
-Classification of airspace A – G
-Controlled airspace
-Uncontrolled airspace
-Prescribed outbound and inbound routes
-Restricted areas
-Weather situation
-Minimum safe altitudes
-Interpret, before every flight, the air traffic control information from AIP and NOTAMS
obtained from AIS, for:
-Departure
-En route
-Destination
-Possible alternative fields
-Select and/or calculate the route, true air speeds, heights and alternate fields, taking into account:
-Prescribed outbound and inbound routes
-Restricted areas
-Weather situation
-Minimum safe altitudes
-Nav. Aids
-Conspicuous points
-Semi circular rules
-Calculate the minimum pressure altitude from MOCA, OAT and QNH
-Calculate how many feet to climb after take off from an aerodrome to a given level
-Find the frequency and ident of a nav. aid from the chart
033 01 01 02 Measurement of tracks and distances
-Find the checkpoints
-Calculate, or obtain from the chart, courses (tracks) and distances to fly
-Draw the intended route in the navigation chart considering:
-Restricted areas
-Danger areas
-Prohibited areas
-Other airspace restrictions
-Find the highest obstacle within a given distance either side of the track
-Derive the following data from the chart and transfer to the navigation plan form:
-Check points and/or turning points
-Distances in NM (using minutes of latitude along a meridian)
-True courses (tracks)
033 01 01 03 Obtaining wind velocity forecast for each leg
-Wind
-At aerodromes
-At cruising levels
-Visibility
-Clouds and cloudbase
-Meteorological hazards
033 01 01 04 Computation of headings, ground speeds, and time en-route from tracks, true airspeed and wind velocities

CRANFIELD AVIATION TRAINING SCHOOL LTD. PART-FCL ATO N° 276
CATS INNOVATION CENTRE, LUTON, Bedfordshire LU2 8DL U.K.   www.catsaviation.com

CATS

1-1   Flight Planning & Monitoring

-Apply the annual change to the charted value of the variation if applicable (not necessary if newest charts are used)
-Transfer the calculated variation to the flight plan form
-Calculate the true air speed at given:
-Flight level
☐Temperature and instrument/position error of the airspeed indicator
☐Calculate the magnetic heading given:
☐The true course
☐TAS and wind vector
☐Calculate the ground speed given:
☐The true airspeed
☐Course
☐Wind speed and wind direction and/or (equivalent) wind component

033 01 01 05 Completion of pre-flight portion of navigation flight log
☐Find departure and arrival routes to be flown
☐Calculate the position of the top of climb (TOC) and top of descent (TOD) by distance and time for given data
☐Calculate the individual leg times and the total time en route
☐Calculate the total time enroute for the trip
☐Identify the omitted course and distance elements for a partially completed flight log
☐Calculate or obtain from the chart those elements and insert them to complete the flight log entries

033 01 02 00 Completing the Fuel Plan
033 01 02 01 Computation of planned fuel usage for each leg and total fuel usage for the flight
☐Compute the planned total fuel usage for the flight by consulting the fuel usage tables and/or graphs from the pilots operating handbook in addition to the navigation plan for times enroute
☐Find the maximum distance to fly given appropriate data

033 01 02 02 Fuel for holding or diversion to alternate airfield
☐State the definition of the alternate and final reserve fuel and the requirements for aeroplanes with reciprocating and turbine engines
☐Define final reserve fuel
☐Obtain and calculate the final reserve fuel for holding
☐Obtain the fuel for flying from the destination to the alternate from the appropriate fuel table or graph

033 01 02 03 Reserves
☐Define the unforeseen items for which contingency fuel is to be carried
☐State and explain the requirements for contingency fuel for small aircraft as detailed in JAR-OPS
☐Calculate the contingency fuel
☐State and/or explain the components of the reserve fuel
☐Explain that additional fuel is required in special circumstances when the trip fuel, contingency fuel, alternate fuel and final reserve fuel are not sufficient for:
☐Holding at 1500 ft (450 m) above the airfield in ISA conditions
☐An engine failure and/ or depressurization at the critical point between alternates and/or destination
☐Calculate the additional fuel if necessary

033 01 02 04 Total fuel requirements for flight
☐Calculate the block fuel for a flight including :
☐Taxi fuel depending on
☐Aerodrome
☐Type of aircraft
☐Trip fuel
☐Contingency fuel
☐Alternate fuel
☐Final reserve fuel
☐Extra fuel at captains discretion

033 01 02 05 Completion of pre-flight portion of fuel log
☐Complete a fuel log which is presented with some of the elements missing, deriving those items from fuel tables and/ or graphs or other appropriate data

033 01 03 00 Carry out flight monitoring and in-flight replanning
033 01 03 01 In-flight fuel computations
☐Calculate, in flight, the fuel quantities used and remaining at navigational checkpoints

CRANFIELD AVIATION TRAINING SCHOOL LTD. PART-FCL ATO N° 276
CATS INNOVATION CENTRE, LUTON, Bedfordshire LU2 8DL U.K.   www.catsaviation.com

1-2   Flight Planning & Monitoring

033 01 03 02 Calculation of actual consumption rate
☐Calculate the actual consumption rate given:
☐The fuel used
☐The flight time
☐Compare the actual and the planned fuel consumption by means of calculation or flight progress chart
☐Compare the remaining fuel with the actual fuel to be used

033 01 03 03 Revision of fuel reserves estimates
☐Calculate the remaining fuel at a nav checkpoint taking into account the actual fuel flow and the fuel used

033 01 03 04 In-flight replanning incase of problems
☐Perform in flight revision of the fuel plan, if necessary, by:
☐Selecting a new destination
☐Selection of power settings to the old or a new destination
☐Calculating a new time to a new destination with a new ground speed to be calculated with given wind, TAS (true air speed) and course
☐Check the current fuel state, fuel requirements and fuel reserves
☐Explain that, in the case of a flight revision, the commander has to check the traffic and the condition of the new destination airfield and its designated alternate. The commander must also check the meteorological conditions at new destination and designated alternate airfield before the decision to continue the flight to the new destination or alternate. The aircraft must be able to land with the final reserve fuel

033 01 04 00 Radio communication and navigation aids
☐State the frequencies of the various means of Communication and Navigational aids

033 01 04 01 Communication frequencies and call signs for appropriate control agencies and in-flight service facilities such as weather stations
☐Find communication frequencies and call signs for appropriate control agencies and in-flight service facilities, flight information services, weather information stations, Automatic Terminal Information Service stations

033 01 04 02 Radio navigation and approach aids
☐On a route facility chart, locate the radio navigation aids and , from the symbols and other data shown, determine:
☐The type of facility/ service provided
☐Frequency
☐Identification
☐Modulation (as appropriate)

033 03 00 00 PRACTICAL FLIGHT PLANNING VFR
033 03 01 00 Chart preparation
033 03 01 01 Plot tracks and measure directions and distances
☐Find the checkpoints
☐Draw the intended route in the navigation chart taking into account:
☐Restricted areas
☐Danger areas
☐Prohibited areas
☐Other airspace restrictions
☐Find the highest obstacle for 5 NM either side of the track
☐Derive the following data from the chart and transfer to the navigation plan form:
☐Check points and/or turning points
☐Distances in NM by measuring with meridian minutes
☐Courses

033 03 02 00 Navigation plan
033 03 02 01 Completing the navigation plan
☐Complete the flight log with the courses and distances as taken from a chart prepared with routes
☐Derive and calculate the headings using
☐Wind as provided
☐TAS
☐Course
☐Variation

033 03 03 00 Simple fuel plans
033 03 03 01 Preparation of fuel logs showing planned values
☐Prepare fuel log showing the planned values for:

☐Fuel used on each leg considering temperature, distance, flight level and wind
☐Fuel remaining at the end of a flight sector
☐Endurance based on fuel remaining and planned consumption rate at the end of a flight sector

033 03 04 00 Radio planning practice
033 03 04 01 Communications
☐Find the frequencies and call signs of air traffic control agencies and facilities for in-flight services such as weather information

033 03 04 02 Navigation aids
☐Find the frequencies and identifiers of en-route terminal navigation aids which can be used

033 04 00 00 IFR (AIRWAYS) FLIGHT PLANNING
033 04 01 00 Meteorological considerations
033 04 01 01 Analysis of existing patterns alongside possible routes
☐Analyse the weather chart, locate and name the different weather systems on the route such as warm and cold fronts, occluded fronts, depressions, high pressure areas, hurricanes, thunderstorms

033 04 01 02 Analysis of winds aloft along prospective routes
☐Analyse the wind/ temperature for the relevant flight level(s), derive the estimated winds and temperatures along the prospective route for each leg

033 04 01 03 Analysis of existing and forecast weather conditions at destination and possible alternates
☐Analyse the TAF's and METAR's and determine the weather at the departure aerodrome, the destination and the alternates considering the following elements:
☐Wind
☐Visibility
☐Runway visual range
☐Thunderstorms
☐Precipitation
☐Cloud base
☐Temperature

033 04 02 00 Selection of routes to destination and alternates
033 04 02 01 Preferred airways routings
☐Select the preferred airways using the following criteria:
☐Optimum altitude/ flight level
☐AIP standard routes
☐Wind
☐ATC restrictions
☐Shortest distance
☐Obstacles
☐North Atlantic Track system (NAT)
☐Westbound tracks A, B, C, D, E ,F. G or H
☐Eastbound tracks Z, Y, X, W, V, U, T or S
☐domestic routes
☐Define the concepts:
☐Minimum Time Track (MTT)
☐Minimum Cost Track (MCT)

033 04 02 02 Extraction of tracks and distances from RAD/NAV chart
☐Extract the courses and distances from the radio-navigation chart

033 04 02 03 Frequencies and identifiers of en-route radio navigation aids
☐Find frequencies and identifiers of en-route radio-navigation aids from the navigation chart

033 04 02 04 Minimum en-route altitudes, minimum crossing and reception altitudes
☐Derive from the charts and explain the following minimum altitudes
☐The Minimum safe En-route IFR Altitude (MEA)
☐The Minimum Obstacle Clearance Altitude (MOCA)
☐The Minimum Off Route Altitude (MORA)
☐The Minimum Sector Altitude (MSA)
☐The Maximum Authorized Altitude (MAA)

☐The Minimum Descent Altitude (MDA)
☐The Minimum Descent Height (MDH)
☐The Minimum Crossing Altitude (MCA)
☐The Minimum Holding Altitude (MHA)

033 04 02 05 Standard instrument departures (SIDs) and Standard arrival routes (STARs)
☐State the reasons why the SID and STAR charts show procedures only in a pictorial presentation style which is not to scale
☐Derive from the SID and STAR charts the following data:
☐Distances
☐Courses
☐Radials
☐DME distances
☐Frequencies and idents of nav aids and frequencies and call signs for communications

033 04 03 00 General flight planning tasks
033 04 03 01 Checking of AIP and NOTAM for latest airfield and en-route status information
☐Find information from NOTAM's and AIP for:
☐Latest status at the airfield of
☐Nav. Aids
☐Obstructions
☐Special procedures due to maintenance, construction of new buildings
☐Opening hours
☐Changed frequencies
☐En-route status
☐Nav. Aids
☐Changed frequencies
☐Closed airways
☐Activity of restricted, danger- and prohibited areas

033 04 03 02 Selection of altitudes or flight levels for each leg of the flight
☐Select altitudes and FL for each leg of the flight
☐Determine the altitude/FL at which the existent wind component gives the best fuel mileage when mass, TAS and air distance are given
☐Find the fuel mileage penalty when deviation occurs from optimum altitude
☐Select flight levels for each leg of the flight
☐Calculate true altitudes to ensure statutory minimum clearance is attained
☐Calculate minimum safe altitude for flight

033 04 03 03 Application of wind velocity on each leg to obtain heading and ground speeds
☐Obtain heading (T) and ground speed from:
☐Wind vector
☐Course on the chart
☐True air speed

033 04 03 04 Calculation of en-route times for each leg to the destination and to the alternate and determination of total time en-route
☐Calculate the en-route time for each leg to the destination and to the alternate
☐Calculate the total enroute time:
☐Using time per leg
☐Using the total air distance

033 04 03 05 Completion of fuel plan
☐Complete the fuel plan by calculating the following:
☐Taxi fuel
☐Tripfuel
☐Contingency fuel
☐Alternate fuel
☐Final reserve fuel
☐Extra fuel

033 04 03 06 Preliminary study of instrument approach procedures and minima at destination and alternate
☐Explain the reasons for studying the instrument departure procedures, the available approach procedures and

associated minima for both destination and alternate
☐Find a standard instrument arrival route which can be expected for the wind at the destination
☐Find a standard instrument arrival route which can be expected for the wind at the alternate

033 04 03 07 Filling out and filing air traffic flight plan
☐Included in 033 02 00 00

033 05 00 00 JET AEROPLANE FLIGHT PLANNING (Additional Considerations)
☐Explain and apply ETOPS rules
☐Explain and apply decision point procedures

033 05 01 00 Additional flight planning aspects for jet aeroplanes (advanced flight planning)
033 05 01 01 Fuel planning
☐Determine the following fuel amounts:
☐Taxi fuel
☐Trip
☐Contingency fuel graphs
☐Alternate fuel
☐Final reserve fuel
☐Extra fuel for safety or economical reasons
☐Take off fuel
☐Block fuel
☐Compute the distance and/or fuel and/or time for an en-route climb
☐Calculate the fuel flow given the appropriate data
☐Calculate the air distance and fuel consumption for a given leg or route
☐State the reasons for parallel use of both 'manual' and 'computer generated' flight plan
☐Explain that manual flight planning is used as a back up method for computerized flight planning
☐Differentiate between overhead-overhead and the climb-cruise-descent flight planning methods as follows:
☐Determine time and fuel for each phase of flight (climb, cruise, descent)
☐Determine time and fuel in the en-route flight level overhead-overhead:, taking into account the additional for climb and descent
☐Differentiate between fuel calculations with fuel flow against the integrated range procedure as follows:
☐Fuel flow procedure: Determination of the required trip fuel with an average fuel flow for the entire flight
☐Integrated range procedure: Determination of the required trip fuel by determining the trip fuel for specified route sectors, using the nautical air miles flown in these sectors and the integrated range tables
☐Explain the principle of the reclearance procedure or 'decision point' as a mathematical method of planning
☐Explain the two different methods of reclearance
☐Mass reclearance
☐Fuel reclearance
☐State the reason for implementing the reclearance flight plan when the difference between Minimum Take Off Fuel (MINTOF) and the (Allowable Take Off Fuel ALLTOF) is equal or smaller less than the Contingency fuel (CONT)
☐Determine the first possible reclearance(decision) point (using the rule of thumb) , given flight plan and 'reclearance airport'
☐Justify the fuel quantities at RECLPT
☐Justify the fuel quantities for the Minimum Take Off Fuel (MINTOF)
☐Calculate and enter the nav. data from the 'reclearance point' to the 'reclearance airport'
☐Calculate the fuel for the route from the reclearance point to the reclearance airport using the integrated range table
☐Calculate the trip fuel from departure to the reclearance airport
☐Calculate the minimum take off fuel (MINTOF) from departure to reclearance airport
☐Calculate the minimum take off fuel for reclearance
☐Determine the fuel amounts for a flight in accordance with the laid down 'isolated aerodrome' procedure
☐Determine the fuel amounts for an Extended Range Twin engine Operations (ETOPS) flight

033 05 01 02 Computation of critical point (CP), point-of-equal time (PET), point of no return(PNR) and point-of-safe-return (PSR)
☐Compute the distance to the critical point (point of equal time)
☐Compute the time of point of safe return considering a given amount of final reserve
☐Compute the distance of the point of safe return

033 05 02 00 Computerised flight planning
033 05 02 01 General principles of present systems
☐State and describe the advantages and shortcomings of a computer navigation plan

033 06 00 00 PRACTICAL COMPLETION OF A FLIGHT PLAN (navigation plan/ flight log)

033 06 01 00 Extraction of data
033 06 01 01 Extraction of navigational data
☐Obtain the following navigation data from the planning charts, SID charts, STAR charts, instrument approach and landing charts
☐Courses
☐Distances
☐Waypoints
☐Bearings and ranges from beacons
☐Co-ordinates
☐Variation
☐Obstacle heights and elevations
☐Classification of airspace

033 06 01 02 Extraction of meteorological data
☐Obtain and decode the following meteorological data
☐Wind at different and appropriate levels and position of the jetstream
☐The presence of thunderstorms
☐Cloud base and thickness of cloud layers
☐Precipitation
☐Temperatures at different levels
☐Icing conditions
☐Areas of CAT and other turbulence

033 06 01 03 Extraction of performance data
☐From the performance data for the aircraft, determine
☐Top of climb
☐Top of descent
☐Fuel flow
☐True air speed
☐Time/ fuel/ distance for climb and descent
☐Final reserve fuel
☐Alternate fuel
☐Find the short distance cruise altitude, given appropriate data

033 06 01 04 Completion of navigation flight plan
☐Calculate the following parameters to complete the flight plan (navigation plan)
☐The block fuel
☐Total ground distance
☐TAS given appropriate data
☐Identify the time system in which time entries have to be made in operational flightplan forms
☐Define the time of departure
☐Define the arrival time

033 06 01 05 Completion of fuel plan
☐Obtain the following data
☐Time, distance and fuel to top of climb
☐Time, distance and fuel at cruise altitude
☐Time, distance and fuel to top of descent
☐Time, distance and fuel for descent
☐Total time, distance and fuel to destination
☐Fuel required from destination to alternate for missed approach, climb to en-route altitude, cruise descent, approach and landing
☐Final reserve fuel
☐Compute the TAS for en-route at a certain flight level with the aid of a graph or table
☐Calculate traffic load, estimated landing mass at alternate and maximum additional load

033 06 01 06 Computation of CP (critical point), including equi-fuel and equi-time points, and PET (point-of-equal-time) and PNR (point-of-no-return) and PSR (point-of-safe-return)
☐Included in 033 05 01 02

033 06 01 07 Completion of air traffic flight plan
☐Complete an air traffic flight plan for a given aircraft and flight, using the instructions contained in the latest AIC, together with the nominated airways charts.

1.1 Nautical Air Miles

An aircraft flying in still air travels the same distance through the air as it does over the ground. Application of wind requires us to consider true air speed (TAS) and groundspeed (GS).

In a Gas Turbine engine, fuel consumption is based on the flow of air through it and not on distance flown by the aircraft over the ground (Nautical Ground Miles, NGM). This 'air' distance is known as Nautical Air Miles (NAM). There is a relationship between NAM and NGM, which is related to the effect of wind:

$$\text{Nautical Air Miles (NAM)} = \text{Nautical Ground Miles} \times \frac{\text{TAS}}{\text{TAS} \pm \text{Wind}}$$

This formula may be re-arranged as follows:

$$\text{Nautical Ground Miles (NGM)} = \text{Nautical Air Miles} \times \frac{\text{TAS} \pm \text{Wind}}{\text{TAS}}$$

These mathematical formulae are presented in the CAP 697.

There is also a graphical method of converting NAM to NGM (or from NGM to NAM) in the CAP 697 (Figure 4.5.2 wind range correction graph). The graphical method produces less accurate answers hence the mathematical is recommended.

To use the graph in the CAP 697:

1. Enter at the bottom left with the average cruise TAS.

2. Go up to the appropriate wind component, noting headwind / tailwind.

3. Go horizontally to the NGM for the leg in question.

4. Come down vertically to find NAM.

NGM may be found by performing steps 1-3, then going up from NAM to where the lines intersect within the NGM scale.

There is a need to be as accurate as possible when interpolating within the graph.

Other graphs and tables in CAP 697 are annotated to the effect that the distances shown are Nautical Air Miles.

1.2 Wind range correction Graph

CIVIL AVIATION AUTHORITY   DATA SHEET
FUEL PLANNING   MRJT 1

5.2   Wind Range Correction   (Fig. 4.5.2)

This graph is used for conversion of nautical ground miles to nautical air miles. (This is
intended for use in conjunction with the 'integrated range' tables).
Enter graph with average TAS. Correct for wind component.
Move to ground distance at the right then vertically down to read corresponding air distance.
For longer distances than shown on the graph apply a factor of 10 to the tabulated values.

Figure 4.5.2 WIND RANGE CORRECTION GRAPH

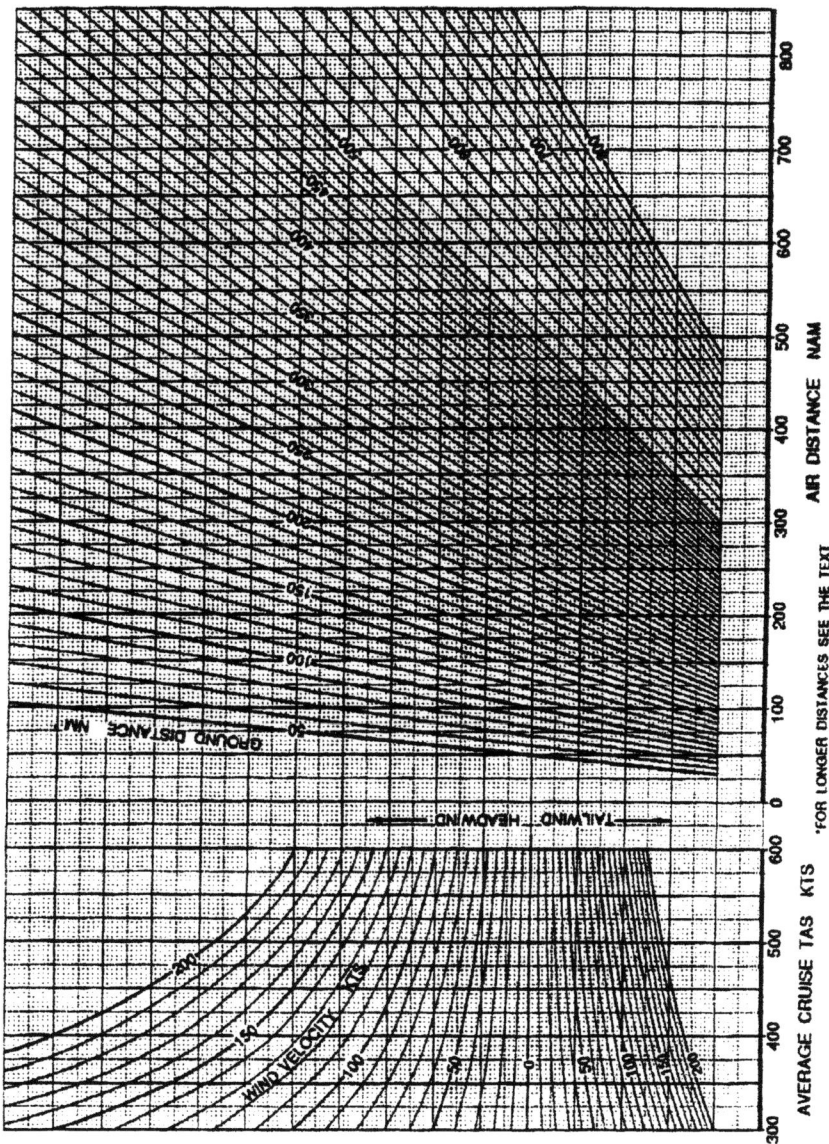

FUEL PLANNING   45

Figure 1.1

CRANFIELD AVIATION TRAINING SCHOOL LTD. PART-FCL ATO N° 276
CATS INNOVATION CENTRE, LUTON, Bedfordshire LU2 8DL U.K.   www.catsaviation.com

Example 1:
Cruise TAS = 400 KT NGM = 250 Still air What is the value for NAM?
Mathematical solution: Nautical Air Miles (NAM) = Nautical Ground Miles x $\dfrac{TAS}{TAS \pm Wind}$ Nautical Air Miles (NAM) = 250 x $\dfrac{400}{400}$ Nautical Air Miles (NAM) = <u>250</u> Gross error check: In still air TAS = GS therefore NAM should be the same as NGM Graphical solution: 1. Enter at the bottom left with the average cruise TAS of 400 KT 2. Go up to the appropriate wind component, noting headwind / tailwind In this case still air is the horizontal line denoted zero 3. Go <u>horizontally</u> to the NGM for the leg in question which is the 250 NGM diagonal line 4. Come down <u>vertically</u> to find NAM of <u>250</u>

Example 2:
Cruise TAS = 400 KT NGM = 250 50 KT headwind What is the value for NAM?
Mathematical solution: Nautical Air Miles (NAM) = Nautical Ground Miles x $\dfrac{TAS}{TAS \pm Wind}$ Nautical Air Miles (NAM) = 250 x $\dfrac{400}{350}$ Nautical Air Miles (NAM) = <u>286</u> Gross error check: In a headwind TAS is greater than GS therefore NAM should be more than NGM Graphical solution: 1. Enter at the bottom left with the average cruise TAS of 400 KT 2. Go up to the appropriate wind component, noting headwind / tailwind In this a 50 KT headwind is the line sloping up to the left denoted 50 3. Go <u>horizontally</u> to the NGM for the leg in question which is the 250 NGM diagonal line 4. Come down <u>vertically</u> to find NAM of approximately <u>285</u>

Example 3:
Cruise TAS = 400 KT
NGM = 250
50 KT tailwind
What is the value for NAM?

Mathematical solution:

Nautical Air Miles (NAM) = Nautical Ground Miles x $\dfrac{TAS}{TAS \pm Wind}$

Nautical Air Miles (NAM) = 250 x $\dfrac{400}{450}$

Nautical Air Miles (NAM) = <u>222</u>

Gross error check: In a tailwind TAS is less than GS therefore NAM should be less than NGM

Graphical solution:

1. Enter at the bottom left with the average cruise TAS of 400 KT
2. Go up to the appropriate wind component, noting headwind / tailwind
In this a 50 KT tailwind is the line sloping down to the left denoted 50
3. Go <u>horizontally</u> to the NGM for the leg in question which is the 250 NGM diagonal line
4. Come down <u>vertically</u> to find NAM of approximately <u>225</u>

Self Assessment Test 01

1   Flight planning chart for an aeroplane states, that the time to reach the cruising level at a given gross mass is 36 min and the distance travelled is 157 NM (zero-wind). What will be the distance travelled with an average tailwind component of 60 KT?
A)   128 NM
B)   157 NM
C)   228 NM
D)   193 NM

2   The still air distance in the climb is 189 Nautical Air Miles (NAM) and time 30 min. What ground distance would be covered in a 30 KT head wind?
A)   174 NM
B)   203 NM
C)   188 NM
D)   193 NM

3   A sector distance is 450 NM long. The TAS is 460 KT. The wind component is 50 KT tailwind. What is the still air distance?
A)   511 Nautical Air Miles (NAM)
B)   406 Nautical Air Miles (NAM)
C)   499 Nautical Air Miles (NAM)
D)   414 Nautical Air Miles (NAM)

CRANFIELD AVIATION TRAINING SCHOOL LTD. PART-FCL ATO N° 276
CATS INNOVATION CENTRE, LUTON, Bedfordshire LU2 8DL U.K.
CATS
www.catsaviation.com
1-12
Flight Planning & Monitoring

Self Assessment Test 01 Answers

1	D
2	A
3	B

CRANFIELD AVIATION TRAINING SCHOOL LTD. PART-FCL ATO N° 276
CATS INNOVATION CENTRE, LUTON, Bedfordshire LU2 8DL U.K.

www.catsaviation.com

1-13

Flight Planning & Monitoring

CHAPTER 2
VFR Flight Planning

According to Chapter 17 of Annex 4, the ICAO 1:500 000 Aeronautical Chart provides information to satisfy the requirements of visual air navigation for low speed, short- or medium-range operations at low and intermediate levels. The chart may be used to: serve as a basic aeronautical chart, provide a suitable medium for basic pilot and navigation training and supplement highly specialized charts, which do not provide essential visual information.

2.1 Airspace in which VFR flight is permitted

ICAO Annex 4 states that significant elements of the air traffic services system including, where practicable, control zones, aerodrome traffic zones, control areas, flight information regions and other airspace in which VFR flights operate shall be shown together with the appropriate class of airspace. Prohibited, restricted and danger areas shall also be shown.

VFR flights shall not be flown over the congested areas of cities at a height less than 1000' above the highest obstacle within a radius of 600 m from the aircraft

Class	Type of flight	Separation provided	Service provided	Speed limitation*	Radio communication requirement	Subject to an ATC clearance
A	IFR only	All aircraft	Air traffic control service	Not applicable	Continuous two-way	Yes
B	IFR	All aircraft	Air traffic control service	Not applicable	Continuous two-way	Yes
	VFR	All aircraft	Air traffic control service	Not applicable	Continuous two-way	Yes
C	IFR	IFR from IFR IFR from VFR	Air traffic control service	Not applicable	Continuous two-way	Yes
	VFR	VFR from IFR	1) Air traffic control service separation from IFR; 2) VFR / VFR traffic information (and traffic avoidance advice on request)	250 KIAS below 3050 m (10000') AMSL	Continuous two-way	Yes
D	IFR	IFR from IFR	Air traffic control service, traffic information about VFR flights (and traffic avoidance advice on request)	250 KIAS below 3050 m (10000') AMSL	Continuous two-way	Yes
	VFR	Nil	IFR / VFR and VFR / VFR traffic information (and traffic avoidance advice on request)	250 KIAS below 3050 m (10000') AMSL	Continuous two-way	Yes
E	IFR	IFR from IFR	Air traffic control service and, as far as practical, traffic information about VFR flights	250 KIAS below 3050 m (10000') AMSL	Continuous two-way	Yes
	VFR	Nil	Traffic information as far as practical	250 KIAS below 3050 m (10000') AMSL	No	No
F	IFR	IFR from IFR as far as practical	Air traffic advisory service; flight information service	250 KIAS below 3050 m (10000') AMSL	Continuous two-way	No
	VFR	Nil	Flight information service	250 KIAS below 3050 m (10000') AMSL	No	No
G	IFR	Nil	Flight information service	250 KIAS below 3050 m (10000') AMSL	Continuous two-way	No
	VFR	Nil	Flight information service	250 KIAS below 3050 m (10000') AMSL	No	No

* When the height of the transition altitude is lower than 3050 m (10000') AMSL, FL 100 should be used in lieu of 10000'

Figure 2.1 Classification of Airspaces

2.2 Cruising altitudes

Except where otherwise indicated by air traffic control clearances or specified by the appropriate ATS authority, VFR flights in level cruising flight when operated above 900 m (3000') from the ground or water, or a higher datum as specified by the appropriate ATS authority, shall be conducted at a flight level appropriate to the track as specified in a Table of cruising levels (Annex 2 Chapter 4):

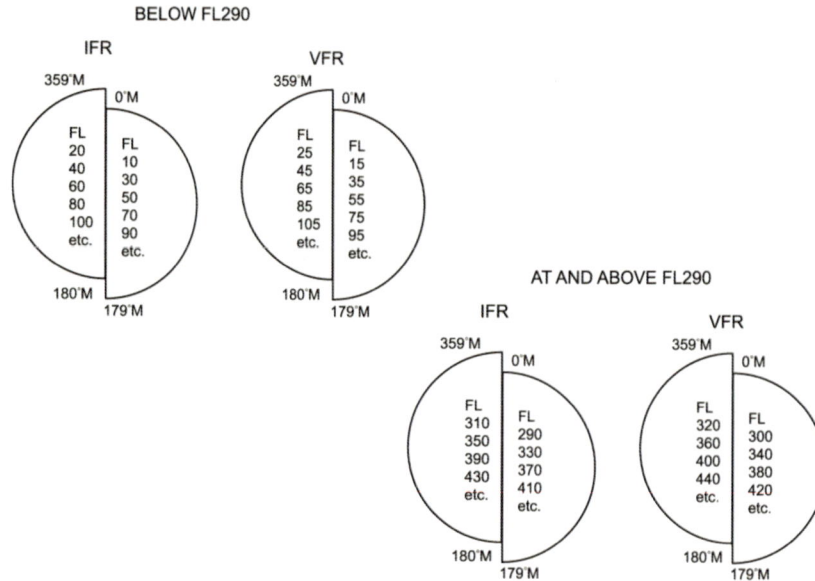

Figure 2.2 Cruising levels

VFR flights shall comply with the provisions for controlled flights:
- When operated within Classes B, C and D airspace
- When forming part of aerodrome traffic at controlled aerodromes
- When operated as special VFR flights

Jeppesen VFR and GPS Chart ED-6 Edition 1999 states

'When planning and conducting a flight under VFR, we recommend maintaining an altitude at or above the depicted MINIMUM GRID AREA ALTITUDES. When below the Grid Area Altitude (during departure and landing) use charts at more suitable scales, e.g. a Visual Approach and Landing Chart or an Area Chart'

Minimum grid area altitudes are shown within each half degree of latitude and longitude. The values provide clearance of all terrain by 1000' in areas where the highest points are 5000' or lower and clear all elevations by 2000' in areas where the highest points are 5001' or higher.

Minimum enroute altitude (MEA) is marked on airways as the first number of the two shown for example for an airway marked 5000 2900a, the 5000 is the MEA whilst the second number 2900a is the off route altitude

2.3   VMC visibility and distance from cloud minima

Annex 2 Chapter 4 states that, except when operating as a special VFR flight, VFR flights shall be conducted so that the aircraft is flown in conditions of visibility and distance from clouds equal to or greater than those shown below:

Airspace class	A***B C D E	F G	
		ABOVE 900 m (3000 ft) AMSL or above 300 m (1000') above terrain, whichever is the higher	At and below 900 m (3000 ft) AMSL or 300 m (1000') above terrain, whichever is the higher
Distance from cloud	1500 m horizontally 300 m (1000') vertically		Clear of cloud and in sight of the surface
Flight visibility	8 km at and above 3050 m (10000') AMSL 5 km below 3050 m (10000') AMSL		5 km**
**	When the height of the transition altitude is lower than 3050 m (10000') AMSL, FL 100 should be used in lieu of 10000' When so prescribed by the appropriate ATS authority:		
a)	lower flight visibilities to 1500 m may be permitted for flights operating:		
1)	at speeds that, in the prevailing visibility, will give adequate opportunity to observe other traffic or any obstacles in time to avoid collision; or		
2)	in circumstances in which the probability of encounters with other traffic would normally be low, e.g. in areas of low volume traffic and for aerial work at low levels		
b)	HELICOPTERS may be permitted to operate in less than 1500 m flight visibility, if manoeuvred at a speed that will give adequate opportunity to observe other traffic or any obstacles in time to avoid collision		
***	The VMC minima in Class A airspace are included for guidance to pilots and do not imply acceptance of VFR flights in Class A airspace		

Figure 2.3 ICAO VMC visibility and distance from cloud minima

Except when a clearance is obtained from an air traffic control unit, VFR flights shall not take off or land at an aerodrome within a control zone, or enter the aerodrome traffic zone or pattern:

- When the ceiling is less than 450 m (1500')
- When the ground visibility is less than 5 km

2.4   Other meteorological factors

On a VFR flight a commander shall not commence take-off unless current meteorological reports or a combination of current reports and forecasts indicate that the meteorological conditions along the route or that part of the route to be flown VFR will, at the appropriate time, be such as to render compliance with these rules possible.

2.4.1   The effect of temperature on altimeter readings

Temperature affects the ceiling height of the aeroplane, making it more difficult to gain the necessary height when the air temperature is high. Cold temperatures reduce true altitude and cause terrain clearance to be reduced. Pressure altimeters are calibrated to indicate true altitude under international standard atmosphere (ISA) conditions. Any deviation from ISA will therefore result in an erroneous reading on the altimeter.

In the case when the temperature is higher than ISA the true altitude will be higher than the figure indicated by the altimeter and the true altitude will be lower when the temperature is lower than ISA

Table III-3-3.   Values to be added by the pilot to published altitudes (feet)

Aerodrome temp °C	Height *above* the elevation of the altimeter setting source (feet)													
	200	300	400	500	600	700	800	900	1 000	1 500	2 000	3 000	4 000	5 000
0°	0	20	20	20	20	40	40	40	40	60	80	140	180	220
-10°	20	20	40	40	40	60	80	80	80	120	160	260	340	420
-20°	20	40	40	60	80	80	100	120	120	180	240	380	500	620
-30°	40	40	60	80	100	120	140	140	160	240	320	500	660	820
-40°	40	60	80	100	120	140	160	180	200	300	400	620	820	1 020
-50°	40	80	100	120	140	180	200	220	240	360	480	740	980	1 220

Note.— The table is based on aerodrome elevation of 2 000 ft; however, it can be used operationally at any aerodrome.

Figure 2.4 Figure 6.5 ICAO Document 8168 Procedures for Air Navigation Services: Aircraft Operations Table III-3-3

2.4.2   Effect of pressure on altimeter readings

Flight towards an area of reducing pressure will cause the altimeter to indicate higher than true altitude

2.4.3   Effect of temperature and pressure on altimeter readings

For both temperature and pressure effects, remember:

From high to low beware below

From low to high you are up in the sky = safety margin

Example:
How many feet do you have to climb to reach FL 75?
Given: FL 75; departure airfield elevation 1500 ft; QNH = 1013 hPa; temperature = ISA; 1 hPa = 30 ft

Flight level 75 = 7500'
Airfield elevation = 1500'
Height to climb = 7500 – 1500 = 6000'

Pressure is ISA
Temperature is ISA

No corrections to 6000'

Answer = 6000'

Example:

How many feet do you have to climb to reach FL 75?
Given: FL 75; departure airfield elevation 1500 ft; QNH = 1003 hPa; temperature = ISA; 1 hPa = 30 ft

Flight level 75 = 7500'
Airfield elevation = 1500'
Height to climb = 7500 – 1500 = 6000'

Pressure is 10 hPa lower than ISA
Temperature is ISA

From high to low beware below

10 hPa = 10 x 30' = 300' difference from ISA
Beware below means your altimeter is over-reading and you are closer to the ground than it displays. In this case by 300'.

Pressure correction to 6000' is –300'

Answer = 5700'

Example:

How many feet do you have to climb to reach FL 75?
Given: FL 75; departure airfield elevation 1500 ft; QNH = 1023 hPa; temperature = ISA; 1 hPa = 30 ft

Flight level 75 = 7500'
Airfield elevation = 1500'
Height to climb = 7500 – 1500 = 6000'

Pressure is 10 hPa higher than ISA
Temperature is ISA

From low to high you are up in the sky = safety margin

10 hPa = 10 x 30' = 300' difference from ISA
Up in the sky means your altimeter is under-reading and you are farther from the ground than it displays. In this case by 300'.

Pressure correction to 6000' is +300'

Answer = 6300'

If temperature deviates from ISA the correction is:

1% of true altitude for every 2.5°C difference from ISA
If colder reduce altitude
If warmer increase altitude

Example:
How many feet do you have to climb to reach FL 75?
Given: FL 75; departure airfield elevation 1500'; QNH = 1013 hPa; temperature = ISA –10°C
Flight level 75 = 7500' Airfield elevation = 1500' Height to climb = 7500 – 1500 = 6000' Pressure is ISA Temperature is –10°C colder than ISA
From high to low beware below
–10°C / 2.5°C = 4 = 4% difference from ISA 4% x 6000' = 240' Beware below means your altimeter is over-reading and you are closer to the ground than it displays. In this case by 240'. Pressure correction to 6000' is –240' Answer = <u>5760'</u>

Example:
An aircraft, following a 215° true track, must fly over a 10600' obstacle with a minimum obstacle clearance of 1500'. Knowing the QNH received from an airport close by, which is almost at sea-level, is 1035 and the temperature is ISA -15°C, the minimum IFR flight level will be (Use 1 hPa = 30'):
10600' obstacle + 1500' = 12100' minimum ISA altitude Pressure is 22 hPa higher than ISA 22 hPa = 22 x 30' = 660' difference from ISA Up in the sky means your altimeter is under-reading and you are farther from the ground than it displays. In this case by 660'. Pressure correction to 12100' is +660' Answer = <u>12760'</u>
From low to high you are up in the sky = safety margin
From high to low beware below
Temperature is –15°C colder than ISA –15°C / 2.5°C = 6 = 6% difference from ISA 6% x original 12100' = 726' Beware below means your altimeter is over-reading and you are closer to the ground than it displays. In this case by 726'. Temperature correction to 12100' is –726' Pressure and temperature corrections to 12100' are +660' and –726' True altitude = 12034'
Flying West FLs are EVENS Lowest available IFR flight level below FL290 is <u>140</u>

Strong winds over rough or high terrain may cause strong vertical air currents, perhaps requiring increased terrain clearance.

A VFR flight should not be operating in cloud.

Seasonal variations in the appearance of ground features used for visual navigation may be significant. In a cold climate a lake may freeze over and become snow covered. The same lake in a hot country may evaporate in the dry season.

Self Assessment Test 02

1   How many feet you have to climb to reach FL 75?
     Given: FL 75; departure aerodrome elevation 1500 ft; QNH = 1023 hPa; temperature = ISA; 1 hPa = 30'
A)   7800'
B)   6300'
C)   6000'
D)   6600'

2   An airway is marked 4000 2300a. The notation 4000 is the:
A)   maximum authorised altitude (MAA)
B)   minimum holding altitude (MHA)
C)   base of the airway (AGL)
D)   minimum enroute altitude (MEA)

3   An aircraft, following a 215° true track, must fly over a 10600' obstacle with a minimum obstacle clearance of 1500'. Knowing the QNH received from an airport close by, which is almost at sea-level, is 1035 and the temperature is ISA -15°C, the minimum flight level will be:
A)   120
B)   130
C)   150
D)   140

4   VFR flights shall not be flown over the congested areas of cities at a height less than
A)   1000' above the highest obstacle within a radius of 600 m from the aircraft
B)   2000' above the highest obstacle within a radius of 600' from the aircraft
C)   500' above the highest obstacle
D)   the highest obstacle

CRANFIELD AVIATION TRAINING SCHOOL LTD. PART-FCL ATO N° 276
CATS   **CATS INNOVATION CENTRE, LUTON, Bedfordshire LU2 8DL U.K.**   www.catsaviation.com

2-9   Flight Planning & Monitoring

Self Assessment Test 02 Answers

1	B
2	D
3	D
4	A

CHAPTER 3
IFR Flight Planning

3.1   General Considerations

Annex 6 Paragraph 7.2 states:
An aeroplane shall be provided with navigation equipment which will enable it to proceed:
a)   in accordance with it's operational flight plan;
b)   in accordance with prescribed RNP types; and
c)   in accordance with the requirements of air traffic services;
except when, if not so prescribed by the appropriate authority, navigation for flights under the visual flight rules is accomplished by visual reference to landmarks.
Annex 6 Paragraph 4.2.7.1 states:
The State of the Operator shall require that the operator establish aerodrome operating minima for each aerodrome to be used in operations, and shall approve the method of determination of such minima. Such minima shall not be lower than any that may be established for such aerodromes by the State in which the aerodrome is located, except when specifically approved by that State.
JAR-OPS 1.335:
On an IFR flight, a commander shall not (1) commence take-off; nor- c) continue towards the planned destination aerodrome unless the latest information available indicates that, at the expected time of arrival, the weather conditions at the destination, or at least one destination alternate aerodrome, are at or above the planning applicable aerodrome operating minima.

3.2   Preferred Airways Routings

Preferred airways can be defined by different criteria, these being:
1.   Optimum altitude for most economical fuel usage;
2.   Most direct routeing;
3.   Meteorological conditions;
4.   Topography, for example the Alps;
5.   Air Traffic conditions;
6.   Aeronautical Information Publication Standard Routes;
7.   Polar Track Structure;
8.   North Atlantic Track System.

With respect to altitude and most direct routeing, pilots will tend to find themselves confined by the ATC restrictions. When we look at charts used for airways flying, we see that the availability of certain airways can be restricted for different reasons, be it due to the geographical location (such as the English Channel, with traffic to and from the oceanic entry/exit points of the NAT MNPS airspace) or to control the daily and often predictable flow of scheduled air traffic.

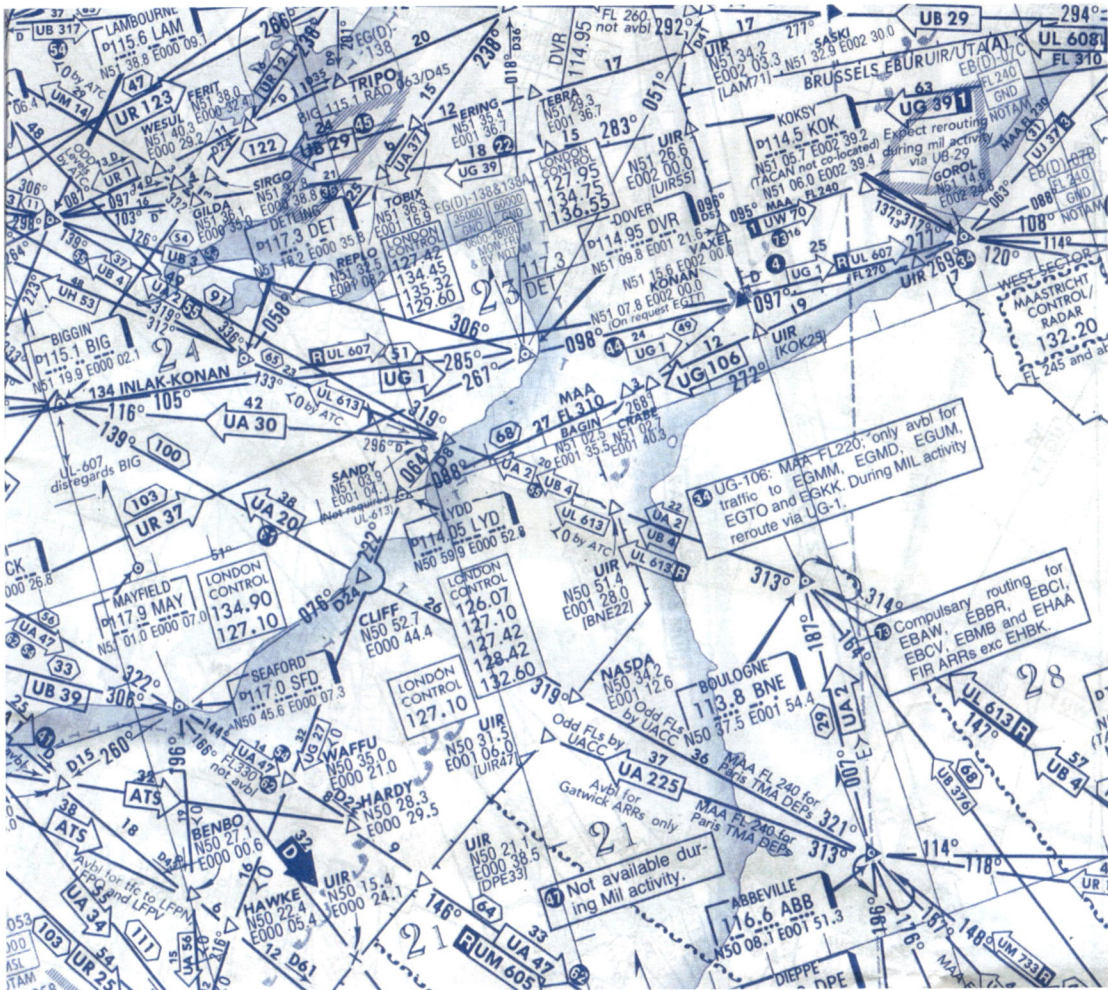

Figure 3.1 Extract from Jeppesen Europe High Altitude Enroute Chart E(HI)4.

In Figure 3.1, the airway UA225 from Abbeville VOR/DME (N5008.1 E00151.3) is only available for flights to Gatwick and both it and UA20 have altitude restrictions of Flight Level 240 if coming from the Paris TMA. By virtue of note 36 at KOKSY VOR/DME (N5105.7 E00239.2), there are limitations put on the use of airway UG106, likewise UW70 is compulsory for some flights.

Some route choices are restricted by the nature of the area. For flights from Europe to South America for instance, the airway network is not as extensive as in parts of Europe. The choice of airway will therefore be limited, more so when the routes are operated by an aircraft which is affected by ETOPS.

Figure 3.2 shows how the many airways routings to the Islands of Tenerife and Fuerteventura reduce to just three (UR1, UB602 and UA32) for the onward journey to Buenos Aires or Sao Paulo.

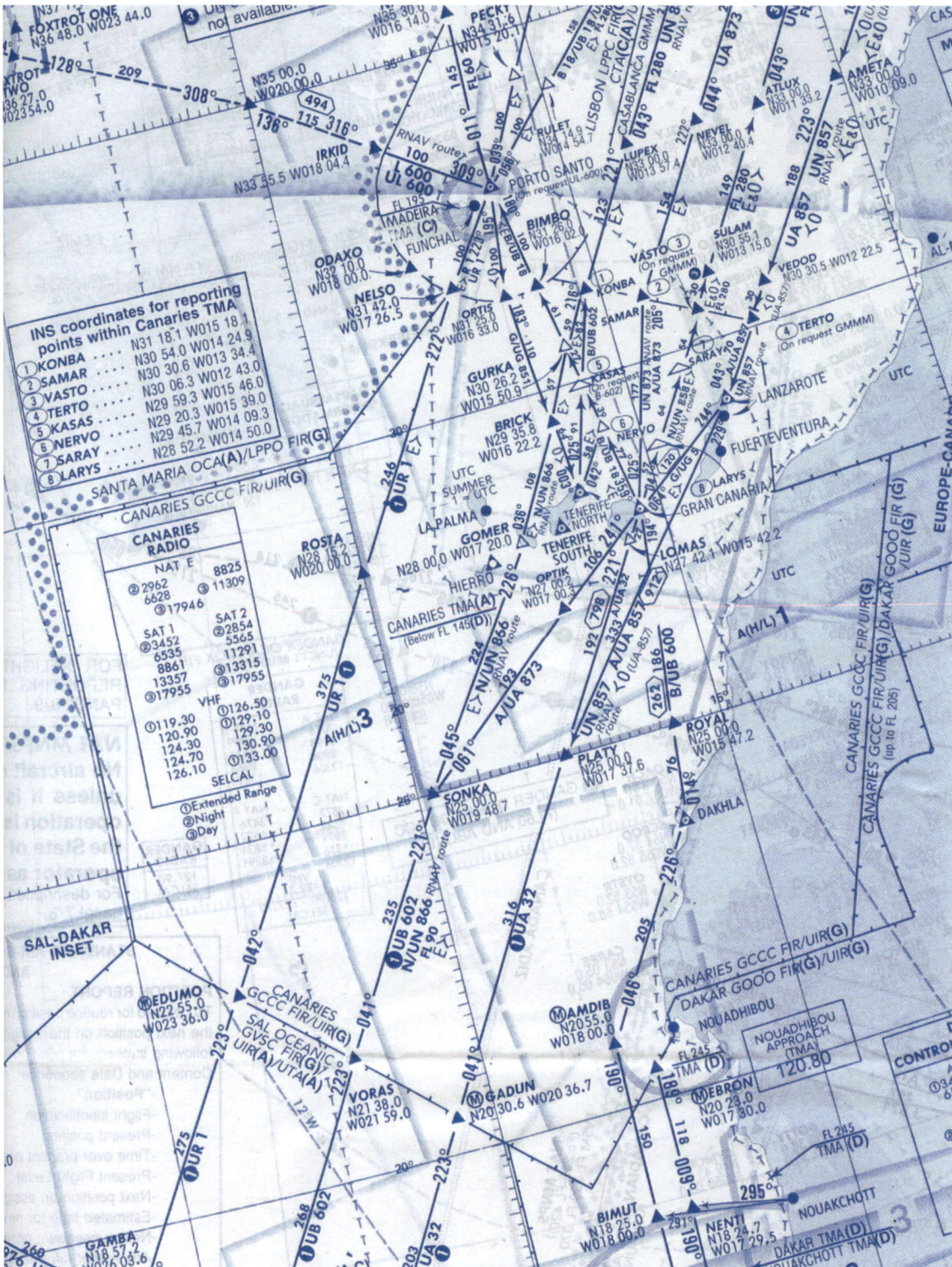

Figure 3.2 Extract from Jeppesen Atlantic Orientation Chart 2AT(H/L)

![CATS logo] **CRANFIELD AVIATION TRAINING SCHOOL LTD. PART-FCL ATO N° 276**
CATS INNOVATION CENTRE, LUTON, Bedfordshire LU2 8DL U.K.

www.catsaviation.com

3-3

Flight Planning & Monitoring

3.3 Polar Track Structure

With the range of aircraft increasing and the reliability of gas turbine engines being proved daily, the shortest routes to places such as San Francisco on the west coast of the United States or direct flights to Japan from the UK are over or near the North Pole. Again, to facilitate this so as to co-ordinate safe passage in these inhospitable areas, a system of tracks has been set up under the control of Reykjavik in Iceland and Bodo in Norway, contained mainly within MNPS airspace. We will cover these tracks in detail later when we look at Grid navigation techniques, but it is important to be aware of them at this stage.

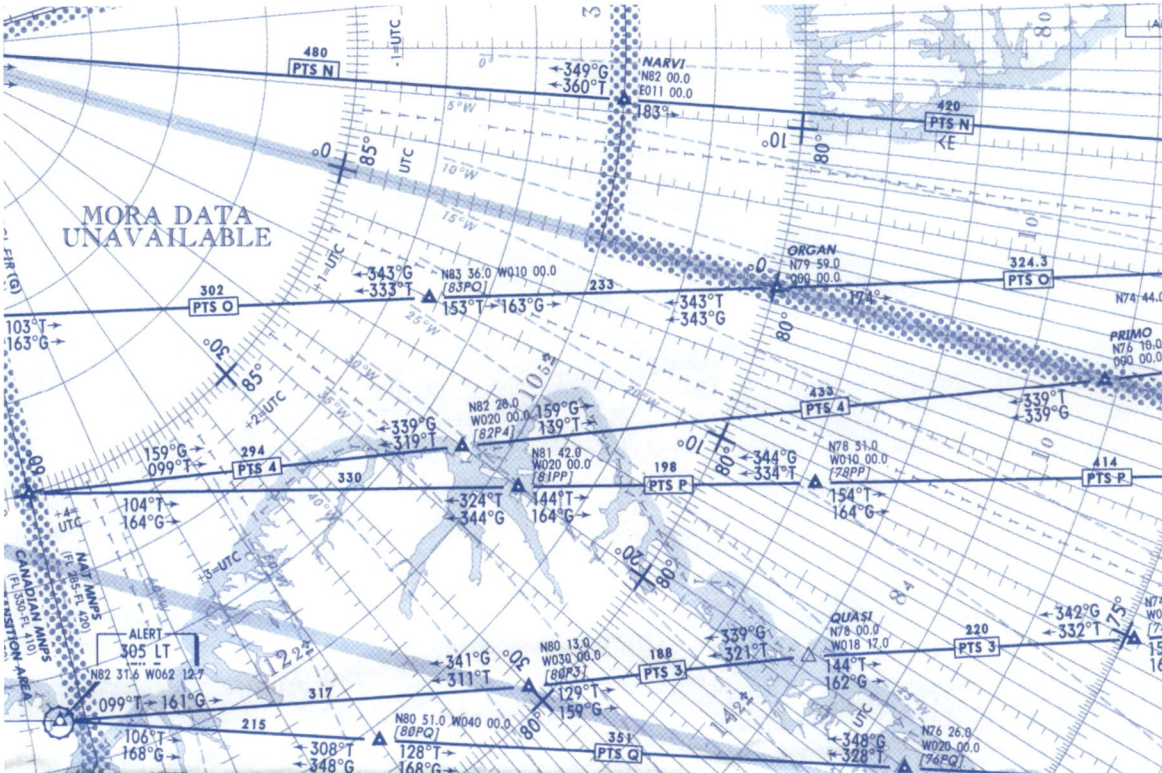

Figure 3.3 Extract of Jeppesen Atlantic Polar High Altitude En-route Chart 5AT(HI)

3.4 North Atlantic Track System

One of the busiest pieces of airspace is that over the North Atlantic. There are approximately 300 individual operations at any one point in time during peak hours.

The eastbound flow is predominantly a night time phenomena and the westbound the opposite, which gives rise to two distinct and separate traffic flows.

One of the prime objectives of any flight in any airspace is to avoid the areas of strongest head wind while seeking the areas of greatest tail wind. Over the North Atlantic the predominantly westerly winds are found to be at the middle latitudes, 50°N to 55°N. As a consequence of this the westbound flow will normally fly north or south of this area and the eastbound flow will attempt to fly through it.

Naturally this does not happen on a daily basis but in general this is the hypothesis, which led to the establishment of the organised track system.

> The North Atlantic organised track system operates twice during each 24-h period with a westbound system operational from 1130 h to 1800 h UTC and an eastbound system operational between 0100 h and 0800 h UTC.
>
> These published times refer to when the flight is going to cross the 030°W meridian of longitude the boundary point between the Shanwick and Gander Oceanic Control Areas, the areas through which the majority of flights transit.

Each North Atlantic Organised Track is identified by a letter.

The westbound tracks begin with the letter "A" as the most northerly track and continue south with "B", "C", "D", and so on depending on how many tracks are needed to accommodate the forecast traffic. Figure 3.4 illustrates a typical distribution of westbound tracks.

The eastbound tracks begin with "Z" as the most southerly track and continue north with "Y", "X", "W" etc. Figure 3.5 illustrates a typical distribution of eastbound tracks.

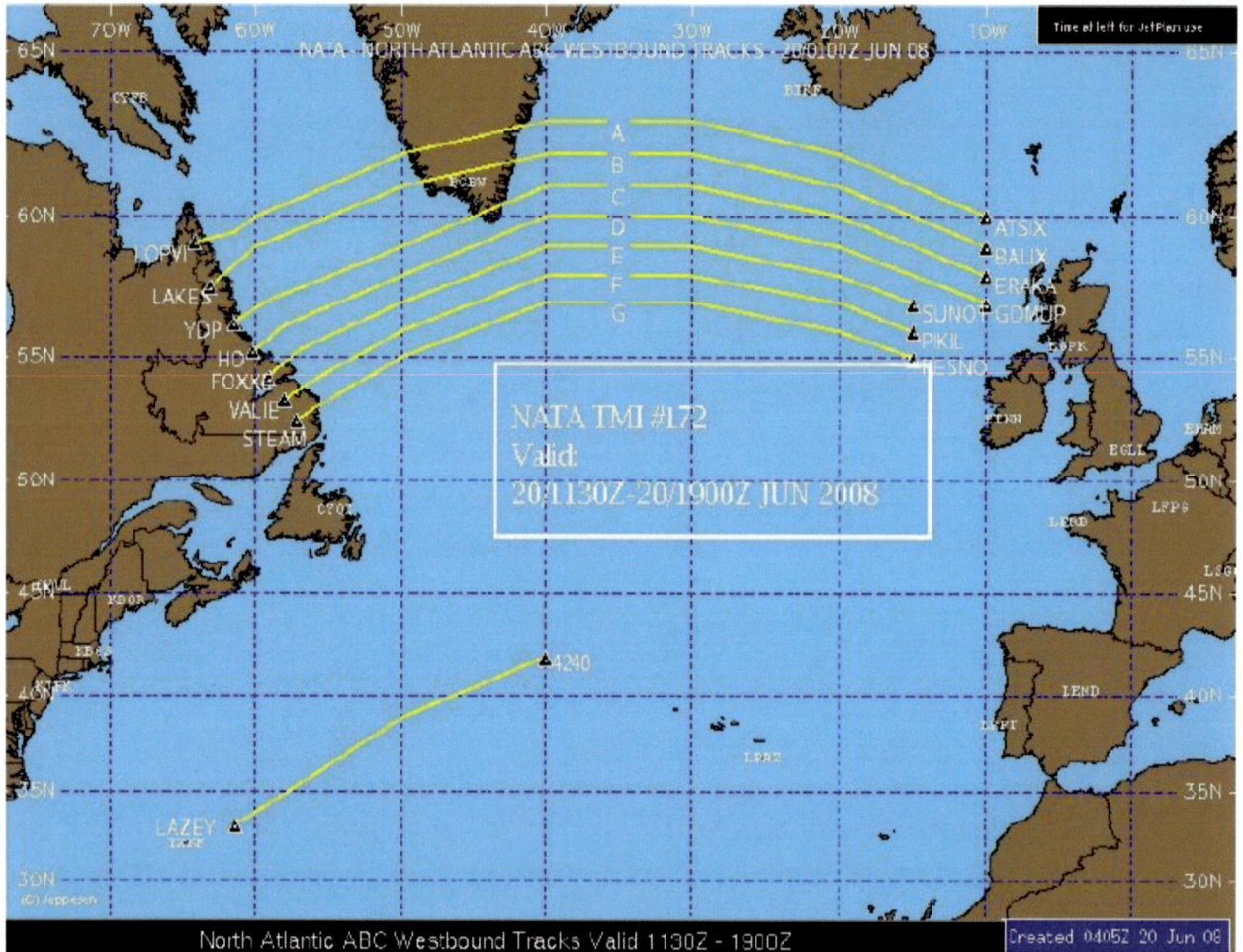

Figure 3.4

CRANFIELD AVIATION TRAINING SCHOOL LTD. PART-FCL ATO N° 276
CATS INNOVATION CENTRE, LUTON, Bedfordshire LU2 8DL U.K.

www.catsaviation.com

3-5

Flight Planning & Monitoring

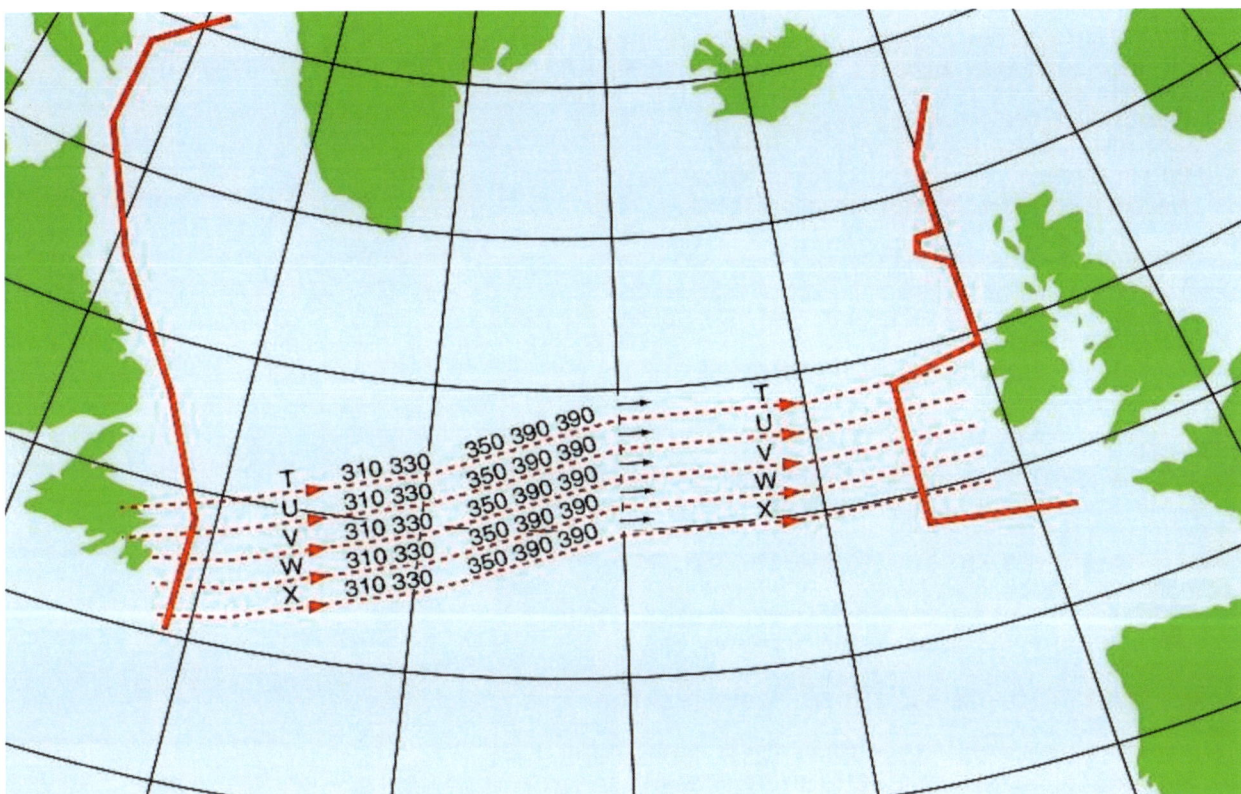

Figure 3.5

The location of these tracks is adjusted (by ATC) on a daily basis in such a way that westbound flights are routed to avoid the strongest adverse winds while eastbound routings take advantage of any tail winds. These adjustments are made without loss of the essential traffic separation criteria.

Messages, known as NAT Tracks, are issued daily and give full details of the applicable NAT tracks system. An extract from a NAT OTS Track message is shown at Figure 3.6 illustrating the west bound track message.

The objective of the NAT OTS is that flights in the appropriate direction should use the tracks and the flight levels specified in the daily NAT OTS message in order to provide safe and optimum separation.

THAT MNPS APPROVAL IS REQUIRED TO FLY IN THIS AIRSPACE.
IN ADDITION, RVSM APPROVAL IS REQUIRED TO FLY WITHIN THE NAT
REGIONS BETWEEN FL310 AND FL390 INCLUSIVE. PLEASE REFER TO
CANADIAN NOTAM 990099 OR A1501/99.

4. 80 PERCENT OF GROSS NAVIGATIONAL ERRORS OCCUR AFTER A REROUTE.
ALWAYS CARRY OUT WAYPOINT CROSS CHECKS.

END OF PART TWO OF TWO PARTS)
(NAT-1/2-
TRACKS FLS310/390 INCLUSIVE MAY 14/1130Z TO MAY 14/1800Z
PART ONE OF TWO PARTS-
A 56/10 58/20 59/30 59/40 58/50 PORGY HO
EAST LVLS NIL
WEST LVLS 310 320 330 340 350 360 370 380 390
EUR RTS WEST 2
NAR N284B N288C N292C N294C N298G N302C N304E N306C N308E N312A
B 55/10 57/20 58/30 58/40 57/50 LOACH FOXXE
EAST LVLS NIL
WEST LVLS 310 320 330 340 350 360 370 380 390
EUR RTS WEST NIL
NAR N264A N270B N272C N274G N276A N278A N280A N282A
C MASIT 56/20 57/30 57/40 56/50 SCROD VALIE
EAST LVLS NIL
WEST LVLS 310 320 330 340 350 360 370 380 390
EUR RTS WEST DEVOL
NAR N242B N248C N250E N252C N254A N256A N258A N260A
D 54/15 55/20 56/30 56/40 55/50 OYSTR STEAM
EAST LVLS NIL
WEST LVLS 310 320 330 340 350 360 370 380 390
EUR RTS WEST BURAK
NAR N220B N228B N230C N232C
E 53/15 54/20 55/30 55/40 54/50 CARPE REDBY
EAST LVLS NIL
WEST LVLS 310 320 330 340 350 360 370 380 390
EUR RTS WEST DOLIP
NAR N202B N206C N210C
END OF PART ONE OF TWO PARTS)
(NAT-2/2-
TRACKS FLS310/390 INCLUSIVE MAY 14/1130Z TO MAY 14/1800Z
PART TWO OF TWO PARTS-
F 52/15 53/20 54/30 54/40 53/50 YAY
EAST LVLS NIL
WEST LVLS 310 320 330 340 350 360 370 380 390
EUR RTS WEST GIPER
NAR N180B N188B N192B
REMARKS.
1. TRACK MESSAGE IDENTIFICATION NUMBER IS 134 AND OPERATORS ARE
REMINDED TO INCLUDE THE TMI NUMBER AS PART OF THE OCEANIC CLEARANCE

Figure 3.6

3.4.1   Interpretation of the NAT OTS message

Control within the MNPS area is divided between five areas namely: Reykjavik, Gander, Shanwick, New York, Santa Maria (Azores). The NAT Track system operates substantially in the Gander/Shanwick areas, which meet at longitude 30°W. Shanwick is the responsible control centre for the area east of 30°W and Gander is responsible for the area west of 30°W. Arising from this division of responsibility and from the fact that there are two distinct traffic flows across the North Atlantic there are two separate NAT OTS messages issued daily.

3.4.2 Eastbound NAT OTS track message

Issued by Gander Oceanic Control Area in the early afternoon UTC and valid for flights flying between North America and Europe during the hours of 0100 to 0800 UTC (at 030°W) the next day.

3.4.3 Westbound NAT OTS track message

Issued by Shanwick Oceanic Control Area around 2300 UTC and valid for flights operating between Europe and North America during the hours of 1130 hours to 1800 hours UTC (at 030°W) the next day.

A careful interpretation must be made of the appropriate NAT OTS message in the following manner:
1.   Confirm it is in the right direction, eastbound/westbound
2.   Confirm that it is for the correct date (calendar)
3.   Confirm the correct oceanic entry and exit points for the NAT OTS track being selected.
4.   Check the eastbound/westbound levels available on this track and confirm that the flight level being selected and filed corresponds to one of these levels.
5.   Confirm the track message number is printed on the track message.

3.4.4 Preferred Route Message (PRM)

Under the procedures for operating in the MNPS airspace and flying on the NAT OTS route system, operators are encouraged to submit in advance the number of flights and their company preferred route for these flights through the appropriate oceanic controlled areas. This assists these authorities in the compilation of the NAT OTS for the particular time period in the following 24 hours. The PRM will normally take into account the "minimum time route" (MTR) which we looked at earlier. For eastbound flights the PRM should reach the Gander OCA by 1100 UTC and at Prestwick OCA by 2200 for the westbound operations.

When subsequently the NAT OTS scheme for the eastbound or westbound flights is published approximately nine hours prior to the commencement of the track system that set of tracks is unique to that period in the 24 hours and may never occur again. This is because it is essentially based on the number of flights in either direction during that time period and on the forecast winds pertinent to those flight operations.

3.4.5 Flight planning on the NAT OTS

While it is not mandatory for flights operating during the time periods of the OTS to plan on a published track it is nevertheless highly recommended that flights do so in the interests of safety and efficient allocation of tracks and flight levels.

A typical flight planning process in a westerly direction during the period of validity of the NAT OTS takes the following form:
•   The flight operations officer/flight dispatcher would initially request from the flight planning computer a minimum time route (MTR) track between the scheduled points of departure and arrival.
•   Having scrutinised this routing across the North Atlantic in comparison with the routes promulgated on the NAT OTS message he/she would then request a flight plan on the NAT OTS track most closely approximating to the north and south of the original MTR routing.
•   Forming part of the request to the flight planning computer would be a specification that the flight plan be created based on the estimated zero fuel mass (EZFM) or the maximum allowable mass (MTOM) should there be performance limitations or restrictions at the departure or arrival runway.
•   The flight-planning computer would then automatically select the optimum cruising flight level on both the MTR and the two NAT OTS track flight plans. Upon receipt of these plans the flight operations officer (FOO)/Dispatcher would ensure that the levels selected were in accordance with those promulgated on the NAT OTS track message.
•   Finally, the FOO/dispatcher either on his own authority or after consultation with the commander would select one or other of the NAT OTS flight plans, as the optimum flight plan for the flight and this would

then be filed with the appropriate air traffic control authorities. Factors that could influence which particular flight plan was chosen could be forecast en route weather such as clear air turbulence (CAT), thunderstorms or significant high level wind shear and also the exit point at the end of the NAT OTS track and its designated North American Route (NAR).

3.4.6   *Random routings during the operating times of the NAT OTS*

While it is not mandatory that flights must plan on one of the specified tracks appropriate to its direction of flight and at one of the assigned flight levels it is highly recommended. Operators who habitually plan flights on "random routes" will obviously pose a difficulty by wishing to fly across the published tracks at the same levels as the aircraft using the tracks.

However, due to commercial requirements, company policy, or a destination lying outside the general group of destinations being served by aeroplanes using the NAT OTS system, a random route flight may be necessary. Such a route will not be refused clearance but, in the majority of cases, will be assigned an uneconomic flight level below those of the aeroplanes on the tracks or will be re-routed to avoid the track system altogether. Either of these will incur a large economic penalty.

3.4.7   *Selection of routes*

Notwithstanding the existence and operation of the NAT OTS system there will be times when flights will be operating in the opposite direction and causing a potential conflict. There are three scenarios for consideration here:

3.4.8   *Flights wholly outside the NAT OTS*

Flights operating wholly outside the NAT OTS obviously do not cause any conflict and therefore may file any route at any flight level the operator wishes.

3.4.9   *Flights joining the OTS from a point outside the NAT OTS*

Two typical examples of this situation are flights from the west coast of North America or Canada to Europe, and flights from Latin America or the Caribbean. In both these cases the departure point of these flights is well outside the westerly entry/exit points to the NAT OTS system.

In the Polar flight case the aeroplane is coming down from the far northern areas of Canada to a point approximately south of the southern tip of Greenland and then continuing in a south-easterly or easterly direction towards the European Continent.

Somewhere around 40°W these flights will come in contact with the northern extremities of the NAT OTS system. The recommendation from the Oceanic Control Authorities is that these flights join the NAT OTS at the closest major reporting point of the most northerly NAT OTS, at an appropriate flight level.

In the case of the flights from the Caribbean/Latin America the recommendation is that they plan to join the most southerly NAT OTS track at an appropriate major reporting point, and flight level.

3.4.10   *Flights leaving the NAT OTS*

Flights leaving Europe and heading towards the Caribbean/Latin America or towards western Canada/USA will, in most cases, due to the geographical location of their departure point, find it most efficient to commence their operation along the most southerly or northerly NAT OTS. They will then leave this route at an appropriate major reporting point when turning away towards their destination.

As with most things in life there are always exceptions and the exception in these cases are Polar Flights. On many occasions the Great Circle or optimum flight route "on the day" will take them across the NAT OTS system at a very early point in their oceanic crossing. In this case the recommended procedure is that they stay below the published flight levels of the NAT OTS (on their optimum route) until clear of the most northerly track.

The same applies to flights to the southern Caribbean islands, Latin America and South America where a low level transit is made until clear of the most southerly NAT OTS at which point the aeroplane then can climb without any restriction to its optimum cruising altitude.

3.4.11 *Cruising levels for random routings*

Any flights not operating within the NAT OTS system i.e. from published entry point to published exit point along the full length of the published track, are known as random routings.

Therefore the selection of cruising levels for these flights must also be considered in three scenarios:
• Flights joining the NAT OTS at some point along that track (Polar/Caribbean) initially may plan/file at the most optimum flight level achievable in the initial stages of the cruise portion. Upon joining the NAT OTS the flight must then expect to conform to the published levels operational within the active track system.
• Flights leaving the NAT OTS must initially plan/file and operate at one of the published levels until the point where the flight departs out of the NAT OTS system whereupon it may cruise at whatever level is desirable or achievable at that point.
• Flights that fly north or south of the active NAT OTS system and maintain the minimum lateral separation may plan/file and operate at their own achievable optimum flight level(s) as these flights do not come in conflict with the traffic operating within the track system.

3.4.12 *Significant reporting points in MNPSA*

Flights operating east/west

• For flights operating south of 70°N, the planned tracks shall normally be defined by significant points formed by the intersection of half or whole degrees of latitude with meridians spaced at intervals of 10° from the Greenwich meridian to longitude 70°W.
• For flights operating north of 70°N, the planned tracks shall normally be defined by significant points formed by the intersection of parallels of latitude expressed in degrees and minutes with meridians normally spaced at intervals of 20° from the Greenwich meridian to longitude 60°W.

The distance between significant points shall, as far as possible, not exceed one hour's flight time. Additional significant points should be established when deemed necessary due to aircraft speed or the angle at which the meridians are crossed, e.g.
• at intervals of 10° of longitude (between 5°W and 65°W) for flights operating south of 70°N; and
• at intervals of 20° of longitude (between 10°W and 50°W) for flights operating north of 70°N
However, when the flight time between successive significant points is less than 30 minutes, one of these points may be omitted.

Flights operating north/south

For flights whose flight paths are predominantly oriented in a north-south direction, the planned tracks shall normally be defined by significant points formed by the intersection of whole degrees of longitude with specified parallels of latitude which are spaced at 5°.

3.4.13 *Optimum Track between Significant Points*

As we are all aware the shortest distance between two points on the earth's surface or indeed above the earth's surface is a Great Circle. Therefore when navigation officers and computer analysts measure and load the tracks and distances between significant points for trans-oceanic flights the Great Circle distance is used.

> The Initial Great Circle track will differ from the final heading due to the convergence of the meridian so an intermediate (mean) Track/True is used.

3.4.14 Aircraft separation within MNPSA

Regarding aircraft separation within the MNPSA there are several situations, which must be considered, the three essential ones being vertical, lateral and longitudinal.

3.4.15 Vertical separation

Since its inception vertical separation within the MNPS area including when the NAT OTS system is operative, has been 4000 ft between aircraft flying in the same direction and 2000 ft between aircraft flying in opposite directions on the same track. Separation is based on the standard barometric subscale setting of 1013.2 hPa.

3.4.16 Reduced vertical separation minima (RVSM)

Since 1997 a system of reduced vertical separation has been operational within the MNPS including the NAT OTS where traffic travelling in the same direction are now separated by only 2000 ft on the same track and by 1000 ft between opposite direction traffic. This is only available to aircraft that are suitably equipped and are RVSM approved.

3.4.17 Lateral separation

Originally the lateral separation was 2° of latitude (120 NM) but, because of improved navigation equipment, this has now been reduced to 1° of latitude (60 NM).

3.4.18 Longitudinal separation

Minimum longitudinal separation between turbojet aircraft meeting the MNPS provided that a portion of the route of the aircraft is within, above, or below MNPS airspace shall be:

1. 10 minutes, provided the Mach number technique is applied and whether in level, climbing or descending flight:
a. the aircraft concerned have reported over a common point and follow the same track or continuously diverging tracks until some other form of separation is provided; and
i. at least 10 min longitudinal separation exists at the point where the tracks diverge;
ii. at least 5 min longitudinal separation will exist where 60 NM lateral separation is achieved; and
iii. at least 60 NM lateral separation will be achieved at or before
*   the next significant point (normally ten degrees of longitude along track(s) or
*   within 90 min of the time the second aircraft passes the common point or
*   within 60 NM of the common point, whichever is estimated to occur first; or
2. If the aircraft has not reported over a common point, it is possible to ensure, by radar or other means approved by the State, that the appropriate time interval will exist at the common point from which they either follow the same track or continuously diverging tracks;
3. Between 10 and 5 minutes inclusive, only when it is possible to ensure, by radar or other means approved by the State, that the required time interval exists and will exist at the common point. Additionally, the preceding aircraft is maintaining a greater Mach number than the following aircraft in accordance with the following:

9 min, if the preceding aircraft is Mach 0.02 faster than the following aircraft
8 min, if the preceding aircraft is Mach 0.03 faster than the following aircraft
7 min, if the preceding aircraft is Mach 0.04 faster than the following aircraft
6 min, if the preceding aircraft is Mach 0.05 faster than the following aircraft
5 min, if the preceding aircraft is Mach 0.06 faster than the following aircraft

When a preceding aircraft is maintaining a greater Mach number than the following aircraft, in accordance with the above, and the aircraft will follow continuously diverging tracks so that 60 NM lateral separation will be achieved by the next significant point, the requirement stated in (1)(a)(ii) above to have at least 5 minutes longitudinal separation where 60 NM lateral separation is achieved may be disregarded.

4.   15 minutes between turbojet aircraft meeting the MNPS provided that a portion of the route of the aircraft is within, above, or below MNPS airspace but not covered by (1) or (2) above.

3.4.19   *Flight levels*

The semi-circular rule dictates that above FL 290 the eastbound levels will be 330, 370, and 410 and in the reverse direction 310, 350, and 390.

Due to the amount of aeroplanes transiting MNPS at peak times the necessity arose to utilise "eastbound" levels in a westbound direction and "westbound" levels in an eastbound direction in order to safely accommodate and separate the traffic existing.

This is done by assigning and publishing the allocation of levels as part of the daily NAT OTS track messages.

On the example NAT OTS message (Figure 3.6) track Alpha has flight levels 330 and 370 assigned.

It will also be seen on studying this attached NAT OTS track message that "even" flight levels are also assigned now. This is due to the introduction of Reduced Vertical Separation Minima (RVSM).

3.4.20   *Navigation System Requirements and Failure Procedures*

In order to receive authority for unrestricted operations within the MNPS area an operator must ensure that the aeroplane types to be used are equipped with two independent long-range navigation systems such as Inertial Navigation System (INS), Inertial Reference System (IRS) or Global Positioning System (GPS).

These must be capable of providing the required navigational accuracy without any reference to ground stations or radar assistance.

3.4.21   *Gross Navigation Error (GNE)*

A gross navigation error is defined as a deviation from cleared track of 25 NM or more

These errors are normally detected by means of long range radar as aircraft leave oceanic airspace. 80% of such errors occur after re-routing. You should always carry out a waypoint cross check after loading the FMS with the re-route data.

3.4.22   *Diversion across the NAT OTS*

Should an event occur in flight necessitating a diversion to the nearest adequate en-route alternate while the aeroplane is flying within the NAT OTS, such diversionary action will necessitate a diversion across the NAT OTS system.

As a consequence of the reduced vertical separation minima it will be necessary for the commander to initiate a descent to 500' below its cruising altitude and turn towards the alternate aerodrome to acquire a track separated by 30 NM from its assigned route or track.

This action will put the aeroplane "between" the NAT OTS tracks on either side and between the flight levels being used. E.g. had the aeroplane initially been at 3500' with traffic above and below at 36000 and 34000' respectively the aeroplane will now be at 34500 ft between the tracks. A descent can now be continued to a level below the MNPS whereupon the flight can then route direct with no level restriction to the en-route alternate.

3.5 ETOPS

3.5.1 Concept

Extended Range Twin Operations (ETOPS) has come about due to the increased reliability and economy of large aircraft such as the Boeing 757/767/777 and Airbus A330 series of aircraft. These aircraft do not have the redundancy of the Boeing 747 or Airbus A340, where the mid-Atlantic loss of an engine would diminish 25% of certain systems and propulsion as opposed to 50%.

Certain special criteria have to be met for an operator to be able to conduct ETOPS operations. These concern the aircraft (extra redundancy in certain critical components, Minimum Equipment List etc.), the crew (most operators have an ETOPS course), and flight planning considerations.

3.5.2 Regulations

"An operator shall not conduct operations beyond the threshold distance determined in accordance with JAR-OPS 1.245 unless approved to do so by the Authority and prior to an ETOPS flight an operator shall ensure that a suitable ETOPS en-route alternate is available within the appropriate diversion time."

Appropriate diversion time is known as the "Threshold Distance". Ordinarily, this is fixed at 60 minutes one engine inoperative TAS. 60 minutes is the "Threshold Time".

JAR-OPS 1.245:
"This distance equals one hour's flight time, in still air and standard conditions, at the normal one-engined inoperative cruise speed."

One hour from a suitable airfield for any large twin-jet puts a prohibitive penalty on any trans-Atlantic or trans-Pacific operation. Indeed, the US west coast to Hawaii would be impossible.

JAR-OPS 1.245:
"Any operations planned to fly a twin-engined public transport aeroplane beyond this distance from an adequate aerodrome will be considered to be Extended Range Twin Operations (ETOPS)."

3.5.3 Definitions

"Suitable" and "Adequate" in the above definitions have the following meanings:

An *Adequate* airfield is determined by the operator and would take into account the normal facilities for the operation, aircraft type etc. Also included should be at least one facility for an Instrument approach. Radar would be a minimum facility to achieve this.

A *Suitable* airfield is one selected by the Commander on the day of the proposed operation. This will take into account criteria within the Operations Manual, NOTAMS as to the serviceability of navigation aids etc. plus:

JAR-OPS 1.297(d):

"An operator shall not select an aerodrome as an ETOPS en-route alternate aerodrome unless the appropriate weather reports or forecasts, or any combination thereof, indicate that, during a period commencing 1 hour before and ending 1 hour after the expected time of arrival at the aerodrome, the weather conditions will be at or above the planning minima prescribed…, and in accordance with the operator's ETOPS approval."

3.5.4   ETOPS Clearance

The Authority will initially clear an operator for 90 minutes ETOPS and then, upon evidence provided by monitoring, successively to 120, 138 and 180 min ETOPS, as required by the operator, dependent on their route structure.

3.6   Other meteorological considerations

Annex 6 Paragraph 6.8 states:

"All aeroplanes shall be equipped with suitable anti-icing and/or de-icing devices when operated in circumstances in which icing conditions are reported to exist or are expected to be encountered."

Self Assessment Test 03

1   Refer to Route Manual chart E(HI)4 CAA-Edition. Aeroplanes intending to use airway UR14 should cross GIBSO intersection (50°45'N 002°30'W) at or above:
A)   FL140
B)   FL160
C)   FL200
D)   FL250

2   An appropriate flight level for IFR flight in accordance with semi-circular height rules on a magnetic course of 200° is:
A)   FL300
B)   FL310
C)   FL320
D)   FL290

3   An IFR flight is planned outside airways on a course of 235° magnetic. The minimum safe altitude is 7800 ft. Knowing the QNH is 995 hPa, the minimum flight level you must fly is:
A)   85
B)   80
C)   100
D)   90

4   An aeroplane is on an IFR flight. The flight is to be changed from IFR to VFR. Is it possible?
A)   Yes, the pilot in command must inform ATC using the phrase "cancelling my IFR flight"
B)   No, you have to remain IFR in accordance to the filed flight plan
C)   No, only ATC can order you to do this
D)   Yes, but only with permission from ATC

5   On an IFR navigation chart, in a 1° quadrant of longitude and latitude, appears the following information "80". This means that within this quadrant:
A)   the floor of the airway is at 8 000 ft
B)   the minimum safe altitude is 8 000 ft
C)   the minimum flight level is FL 80
D)   the altitude of the highest obstacle is 8 000 ft

Self Assessment Test 03 Answers

1	D
2	B
3	C
4	A
5	B

CHAPTER 4
Flight plans

AIRLINE TRANSPORT PILOTS LICENCE
(030 00 00 00 - FLIGHT PERFORMANCE AND PLANNING)
033 02 00 00 ICAO ATC FLIGHT PLAN
033 02 01 00 Types of flight plan
☐Indicate the difference between the types of Flight Plan
☐Individual flight plan
☐Repetitive flight plan (RPL)

033 02 01 01 ICAO flight plan
☐Interpret the fixed format of an ICAO flight plan
☐State the reasons for a fixed format of an ICAO flightplan
☐Interpret the information to be given on the flight plan:
☐Aircraft identification
☐ICAO airline ident plus flight number
☐Aircraft registration
☐Flight rules
☐Type of flight
☐Number of aircraft; wake turbulence category
☐Communication- and nav equipment on board
☐Departure aerodrome with 4 letter ident or ZZZZ and name in "other information"
☐Estimate Off Block Time (EOBT)
☐Cruising speed
☐Cruising level VFR or flight level
☐Route with checkpoints, ATS routes, coordinates and/or bearing and range of a nav.aid and FIR boundary crossing points
☐Destination aerodrome, EET, alternate aerodromes
☐Other information REG/, SEL/, OPR/, STS/, TYP/, PER/, COM/, NAV/., DEP/, DEST/, ALTN/ and RMK/ DAT
☐Endurance
☐Persons on board
☐Emergency equipment
☐Aircraft colour and markings
☐Define the concept of the repetitive flight plan

033 02 02 00 Completing the flight plan
033 02 02 01 Information for flight plan
☐Complete the Flight Plan using information from:
☐Navigation plan
☐Fuel plan
☐Operator's records for basic aircraft information
☐Mass and balance records

033 02 03 00 Filing the flight plan
033 02 03 01 Procedures for filing
☐State the earliest and the latest time, prior to the estimated off block time , that a flight plan should be filed with ATC for onward transmission on the Aeronautical
Fixed Telecommunications Network (AFTN)
☐State the procedure, regarding the flight plan, if take-off is delayed

033 02 03 02 Agency responsible for processing the flight plan
☐Name which ATC unit is responsible for:
☐Checking compliance with the format and data conventions
☐Checking for completeness and accuracy
☐Taking action, if necessary, to make it acceptable for ATC
☐Indicate acceptance and/or changes to the operator

033 02 03 03 Requirements of the state concerning when a flight plan must be filed
☐State and explain that there are circumstances in which the flight plan must be filed earlier

033 02 04 00 Closing the flight plan
033 02 04 01 Responsibilities and procedures
☐Define the responsibility in respect to closing the flight plan
☐Indicate the time limit within which the flight plan should be closed

033 02 04 02 Processing agency
☐Name the agency responsible for processing the flight plan

033 02 04 03 Checking slot time
☐Define the concept slot time/ calculated take off time delivered by the Central Flow Management Unit (CFMU)

033 02 05 00 Adherence to flight plan
033 02 05 01 Tolerances allowed by the stare for various types of flight plans
☐State that there are differences between national regulations and practices and the international standards for rules of the air (candidates are not expected to know these differences)
☐List the publications where the differences can be found
☐List the subjects on which differences can occur

033 02 05 02 In-flight amendment of flight plan
☐List the items of the flight plan which, if necessary, can be changed or amended in the air:
☐State who is responsible for filing an amendment
☐State to which ATC unit that amendment should be communicated
☐Name the maximum divergence of time and/or speed from those given in the filed flight plan before an in-flight amendment should be made

4.1 ICAO Sample Flight Plan

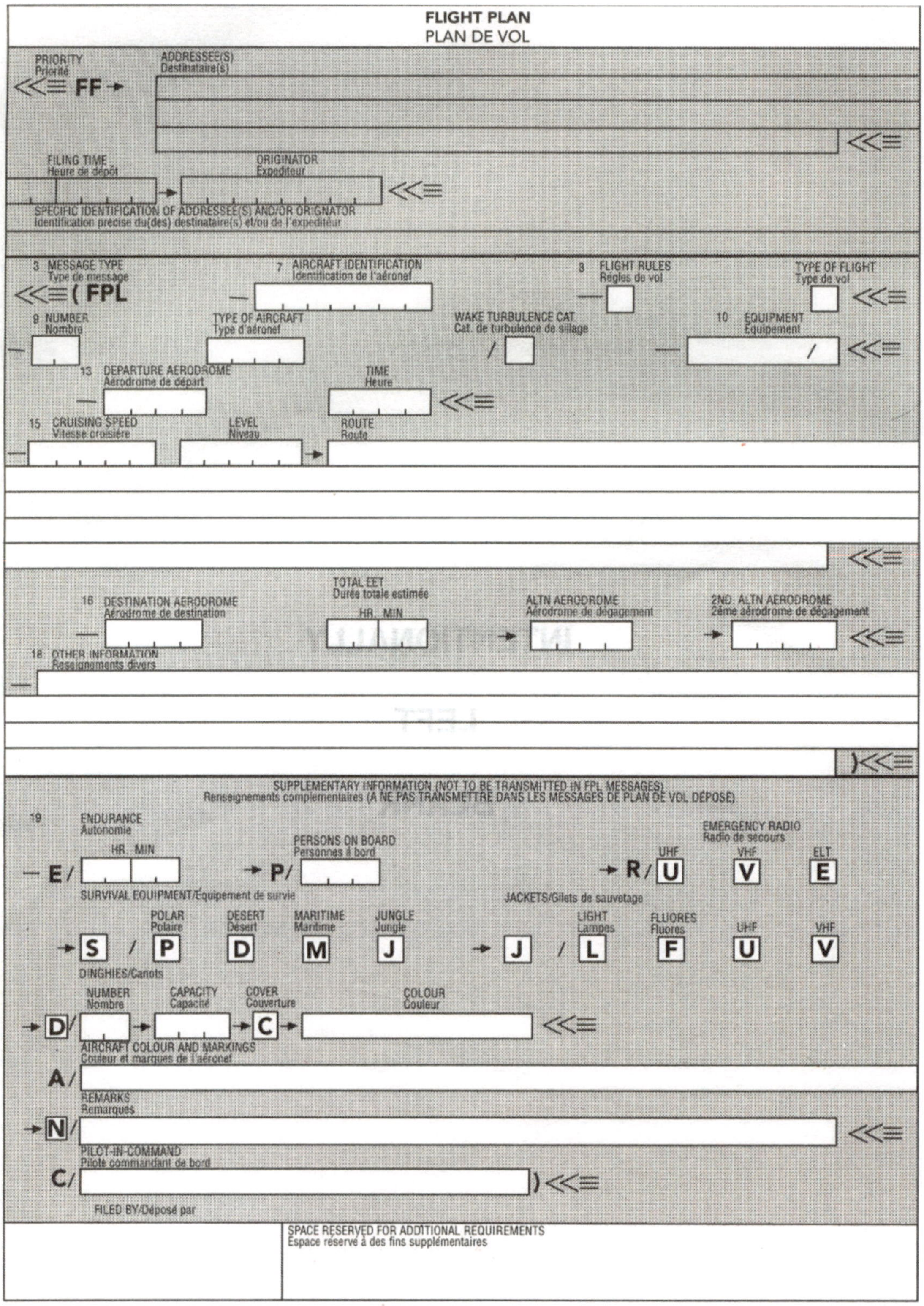
FLIGHT PLAN
PLAN DE VOL

PRIORITY / Priorité — ADDRESSEE(S) / Destinataire(s)
<<≡ FF →
FILING TIME / Heure de dépôt — ORIGINATOR / Expéditeur
SPECIFIC IDENTIFICATION OF ADDRESSEE(S) AND/OR ORIGINATOR / Identification précise du(des) destinataire(s) et/ou de l'expéditeur

3 MESSAGE TYPE / Type de message — <<≡ (FPL
7 AIRCRAFT IDENTIFICATION / Identification de l'aéronef
8 FLIGHT RULES / Règles de vol — TYPE OF FLIGHT / Type de vol
9 NUMBER / Nombre — TYPE OF AIRCRAFT / Type d'aéronef — WAKE TURBULENCE CAT. / Cat. de turbulence de sillage
10 EQUIPMENT / Équipement
13 DEPARTURE AERODROME / Aérodrome de départ — TIME / Heure
15 CRUISING SPEED / Vitesse croisière — LEVEL / Niveau — ROUTE / Route
16 DESTINATION AERODROME / Aérodrome de destination — TOTAL EET / Durée totale estimée HR. MIN — ALTN AERODROME / Aérodrome de dégagement — 2ND. ALTN AERODROME / 2ème aérodrome de dégagement
18 OTHER INFORMATION / Renseignements divers

SUPPLEMENTARY INFORMATION (NOT TO BE TRANSMITTED IN FPL MESSAGES)
Renseignements complémentaires (À NE PAS TRANSMETTRE DANS LES MESSAGES DE PLAN DE VOL DÉPOSÉ)
19 ENDURANCE / Autonomie HR. MIN — E/
PERSONS ON BOARD / Personnes à bord — P/
EMERGENCY RADIO / Radio de secours — R/ UHF U, VHF V, ELT E
SURVIVAL EQUIPMENT/Équipement de survie — POLAR / Polaire, DESERT / Désert, MARITIME / Maritime, JUNGLE / Jungle — S / P D M J
JACKETS/Gilets de sauvetage — LIGHT / Lampes, FLUORES / Fluores, UHF, VHF — J / L F U V
DINGHIES/Canots — NUMBER / Nombre, CAPACITY / Capacité, COVER / Couverture, COLOUR / Couleur — D/ C
AIRCRAFT COLOUR AND MARKINGS / Couleur et marques de l'aéronef — A/
REMARKS / Remarques — N/
PILOT-IN-COMMAND / Pilote commandant de bord — C/
FILED BY/Déposé par
SPACE RESERVED FOR ADDITIONAL REQUIREMENTS / Espace réservé à des fins supplémentaires

Figure 4.1 ICAO Model Flight Plan Form

An operator shall ensure that a flight is not commenced unless an ATS flight plan has been submitted, or adequate information has been deposited in order to permit alerting services to be activated if required.

For the purposes of the Flight Planning and Monitoring examination, you will be using the information contained in the Student Pilot Route Manual. Within the Air Traffic Control section is contained a copy of the

ICAO model Flight Plan form. The instructions for completion of the fields within this form, as laid down in PANS-RAC (Doc 4444), are reproduced in the Student Pilot Route Manual which should be referred to in the examination.

4.1.1   Types of flight plan

1.   Individual.
2.   Repetitive.
3.   Abbreviated. (For that portion under FIR, e.g. Class A airspace penetration.)

4.1.2   Submission of flight plan

A flight plan must be submitted for:
1.   Flights requiring Air Traffic Services.
2.   Flights crossing international borders.
3.   IFR flights.
4.   When required to do so by ATC. (Designated route etc.)

A flight plan may be submitted:
1.   For any flight.
2.   It is advisory for flights over inhospitable territory where search and rescue resources may face difficulties.
PANS-RAC States:
"Except when other arrangements have been made…. A flight plan submitted prior to departure should be submitted to the air traffic services reporting office at the departure aerodrome. If no such office exists at the departure aerodrome, the flight plan should be submitted to the unit serving or designated to serve the departure aerodrome."

A flight plan may be submitted in flight to the Air Traffic Services Unit (ATSU) responsible for the airspace in which the aircraft is flying, but never less than 10 min prior to penetrating controlled airspace.

4.1.3   Submission times

Flight plans should be submitted:
1. Normally 60 min prior to EOBT.
2. Never less than 30 min prior to EOBT.
3. 10 min prior to penetrating controlled airspace if filed in the air.
4. 3 h prior to EOBT for flights requiring Air Traffic Flow Management (ATFM) or Atlantic traffic.

4.1.4   Actions of ATSU accepting

The unit with whom the flight plan is filed will:
1.   Check it for compliance with the format and data conventions.
2.   Check it for completeness and accuracy as far as possible.
3.   Take action if required to make it acceptable to ATSU.
4.   Indicate acceptance or changes made, to the originator.
5.   Onward transmission through the Aeronautical Fixed Telecommunication Network (AFTN) to air traffic units having need of the information.

4.1.5   Clearance

After submission, the following requirements have to be met:

Aircraft requiring Air Traffic Control Service. The aircraft is required to wait for air traffic control clearance prior to proceeding under conditions requiring compliance with air traffic control procedures.

Aircraft requiring Air Traffic Advisory Service. The aircraft is required to wait for acknowledgement of receipt of the flight plan by the unit providing the service.

Clearance can be to the filed destination, or to the Clearance Limit point, beyond which, further clearance will be required (for example, the North Atlantic Track System requires further clearance.)

If the flight is subject to Air Traffic Flow Management (ATFM), clearance may also require a Slot Time, issued by the ATS Central Flow Management Unit (CFMU) in Brussels, to facilitate them in their prime objective:

> Air traffic control units shall issue such air traffic control clearances as are necessary to meet the objectives of collision prevention and the expedition and maintenance of an orderly flow of traffic

4.1.6 Air Traffic Flow Management (ATFM)

The CFMU will issue a Calculated Take Off Time (CTOT), and this is forwarded to the ATSU responsible, who will pass it as part of a flight's clearance. ATC have a slot tolerance of –5 to +10 min, so as to best manage traffic flow. Aircraft Commanders must aim to be ready for departure at CTOT and not to use the slot tolerance for a late departure from the apron.

4.1.7 Departure Delay

For a flight for which a flight plan has been submitted, the flight plan should be amended, or a new flight plan submitted after cancellation of the original flight plan- whichever is applicable- after the following times in excess of estimated off block time (EOBT):

Uncontrolled Flight: After 1 h.

Controlled Flight: After 30 min.

EOBT is defined in PANS-RAC as "the estimated time at which the aircraft will commence movement associated with departure."

4.1.8 Booking out

Booking out does not necessarily mean that a flight plan has been filed on your behalf.

> Rule 20(2) Rules of the Air Regulations 1996 (Air Navigation Order):
> "The commander of an aircraft......departing from an aerodrome.....shall take all reasonable steps to ensure.....prior to departure,....that notice of that event is given to the person in charge of the aerodrome, or to the air traffic control unit or aerodrome flight information service unit at the aerodrome."

Submission of a flight plan satisfies the requirements of Rule 20(2).

4.1.9 In-flight amendments

The appropriate ATSU must be informed by the aircraft commander of the following variations from the filed flight plan:

Inadvertent changes
1.   Variation in flight plan TAS of ± 5%
2.   Change in time estimate. If in excess of 3 min to next reporting point, FIR boundary, or destination aerodrome.

CRANFIELD AVIATION TRAINING SCHOOL LTD. PART-FCL ATO N° 276
CATS INNOVATION CENTRE, LUTON, Bedfordshire LU2 8DL U.K.   www.catsaviation.com

4-5   Flight Planning & Monitoring

Intended changes

1. Change in cruising level:
a) Revised level.
b) Revised TAS.
c) Revised time estimates for FIR boundaries.
2. Change in route, *destination unchanged*:
a) Flight rules.
b) New route, beginning with point of change.
c) Revised time estimates.
d) Other pertinent information.
3. Change of route, *destination changed*:
a) Flight rules.
b) New route, beginning with point of change.
c) Revised time estimates.
d) Alternate aerodromes.
e) Other pertinent information.

4.1.10   Cancellation

An IFR flight can cancel a flight plan when it is intended to continue in VMC and the aircraft is operating outside of airspace necessitating the continued requirement for such a flight plan. This would require transmission to the current ATSU, "(callsign), cancelling my IFR flight". (PANS-RAC 9.1)

The ATSU will have to accept such cancellation, but if they are privy to meteorological information, which would indicate an inability to remain VMC, they will inform the aircraft commander so. (PANS-RAC 9.3)

4.1.11   Diversion

If a flight lands at an aerodrome other than that specified in it's flight plan and no in-flight amendments have been made, the pilot must ensure that the ATSU at the flight planned destination is informed of such an occurrence within 30 min of the flight planned ETA.

4.1.12   Repetitive flight plans

For scheduled operations, where a degree of predictability is inherent, a flight plan may be submitted which will account for the same flight over many days.

Requirements are:
1. IFR flights only.
2. Operated regularly on the same day(s) over consecutive weeks on at least 10   occasions, or every day over a period of at least 10 days.
3. Have a high degree of stability.

A New List (NLST) must be submitted to the CFMU a minimum of 14 days prior to the intended first flight. Any amendments are made by submitting a Revised List (RLST). There must be 7 working days between reception of the RLST and activation of the first flight affected by it. Working days are Monday to Friday, including bank holidays (except December 25th).

4.1.13   Computer flight plans

With regard to computer generated flight plans: a computer can file the ATC flight plan, however should in-flight re-routing occur the computer cannot (within a practicable time) produce a new plan.

4.1.14 *Completed flight plan*

4.1.15 *Nomenclature (International Standards, ICAO Annex 2)*

Filed Flight Plan 'The flight plan as filed with an ATS unit by the pilot or a designated representative, without any subsequent changes.'

Current Flight Plan 'The flight plan, including changes, if any, brought about by subsequent clearances.'

Estimated Off Block Time (EOBT) 'The estimated time at which the aircraft will commence movement associated with departure.'

Estimated Time of Arrival (ETA) 'For IFR flights, the time at which it is estimated that the aircraft will arrive over that designated point, defined by reference to navigation aids, from which it is intended that an instrument approach procedure will be commenced, or, if no navigation aid is associated with the aerodrome, the time at which the aircraft will arrive over the aerodrome. For VFR flights, the time at which it is estimated that the aircraft will arrive over the aerodrome.'

CRANFIELD AVIATION TRAINING SCHOOL LTD. PART-FCL ATO N° 276
CATS INNOVATION CENTRE, LUTON, Bedfordshire LU2 8DL U.K.

www.catsaviation.com

4-7

Flight Planning & Monitoring

Self Assessment Test 04

1 CAS is 130 KT, TAS is 180 KT, GS is 220 KT, the speed box on the flight plan is filled in as follows:
A) N0180
B) K0130
C) K0180
D) K0220

2 Which flights require a flight plan:
1. Any Public Transport flight
2. Any IFR flight
3. Any flight, that is undertaken in regions designated to ease provision of Alerting Service or the operations of Search and Rescue
4. Any cross-border flights
5. Any flight which involves flight over water
A) 1,5
B) 2,4
C) 3,4,5
D) 1,2,3

3 How far in advance of departure time should a flight plan be filed in the case of flights into areas subject to air traffic flow management?
A) 30 min
B) 1 h
C) 2 h
D) 3 h

4 With regard to computer generated flight plans:
1. The computer can file the ATC flight plan.
2. In the event of in-flight re-routing the computer produces a new plan
A) The computer automatically files the flight plan and produces a new one in the event of re-routing
B) The computer can file the flight plan
C) The computer generates a new flight plan in the event of re-routing
D) None of the above are correct

5 A flight plan is considered current when:
A) The ETD is filled in
B) The clearance and any amendments are given and read back
C) The ATD is filled in
D) It is filed

6
The time information which should be entered in box 13 (time) of the flight plan should be:
A) Estimated off block time
B) Time of filing
C) Take off time
D) Engine start time

7 The time information which should be entered in box 16 (total estimated time) is the time elapsed from:
A) Off blocks to on blocks at destination
B) Take off to the initial approach fix of the destination
C) Take off to landing
D) Off blocks to the initial approach fix of the destination

8   In flight plan you enter …….. if the destination airport has no ICAO indicator
A)   / / / /
B)   XXX
C)   ZZZZ
D)   NIL

9   A repetitive flight plan (RPL) is filed for a scheduled flight: Paris CDG to Lyon, Paris CDG as alternate. Lyon airport will be closed at the expected time of arrival. The airline decides before departure to plan a re-routing of that flight to Marseille:
A)   The RPL must be cancelled and a new flight plan for that flight has to be filed
B)   A change to the RPL must be transmitted at least 30 min before the planned time of departure
C)   The pilot-in-command must advise ATC of intention to divert to Marseille at least 15 min before the planned time of arrival
D)   It is not permitted to change destination and the flight must be cancelled

10   If a pilot lands at an aerodrome other than the destination aerodrome specified in the flight plan, ATC at the destination must be informed within …….. of the planned ETA at the destination
A)   10 min
B)   15 min
C)   30 min
D)   60 min

CRANFIELD AVIATION TRAINING SCHOOL LTD. PART-FCL ATO N° 276
CATS INNOVATION CENTRE, LUTON, Bedfordshire LU2 8DL U.K.

www.catsaviation.com

4-9

Flight Planning & Monitoring

Self Assessment Test 04 Answers

1	A
2	B
3	D
4	B
5	B
6	A
7	B
8	C
9	A
10	C

CRANFIELD AVIATION TRAINING SCHOOL LTD. PART-FCL ATO N° 276
CATS INNOVATION CENTRE, LUTON, Bedfordshire LU2 8DL U.K.

www.catsaviation.com

4-10

Flight Planning & Monitoring

CHAPTER 5
Fuel planning for a Single Engine Piston (SEP) aeroplane

5.1   Take off and climb

Fuel carried by a public transport flight must never be less than the minimum required by Appendix 1 to JAR-OPS 1.255 'Fuel Policy'.

Block fuel is defined by Appendix 1 to JAR OPS 1.255 as the total fuel required to operate a route or route segment

Block fuel comprises fuel for:
- Start up and taxi
- Take off and climb to cruise altitude
- Cruise
- Descent
- Alternate/diversion or island reserve
- Holding for a prescribed time
- Landing
- Contingency (Calculated as 5% Trip Fuel)
- Final Reserve (Calculated as 45min at 1500')

Figure 2.1 in CAP 697 enables the calculation of fuel for take off and climb to cruise altitude.

CRANFIELD AVIATION TRAINING SCHOOL LTD. PART-FCL ATO N° 276
CATS INNOVATION CENTRE, LUTON, Bedfordshire LU2 8DL U.K.

www.catsaviation.com

5-1

Flight Planning & Monitoring

5.2   CAP 697 Fig 2.1

CIVIL AVIATION AUTHORITY

FLIGHT PLANNING & MONITORING

DATA SHEET

SEP 1

FIGURE 2.1   TIME FUEL AND DISTANCE TO CLIMB

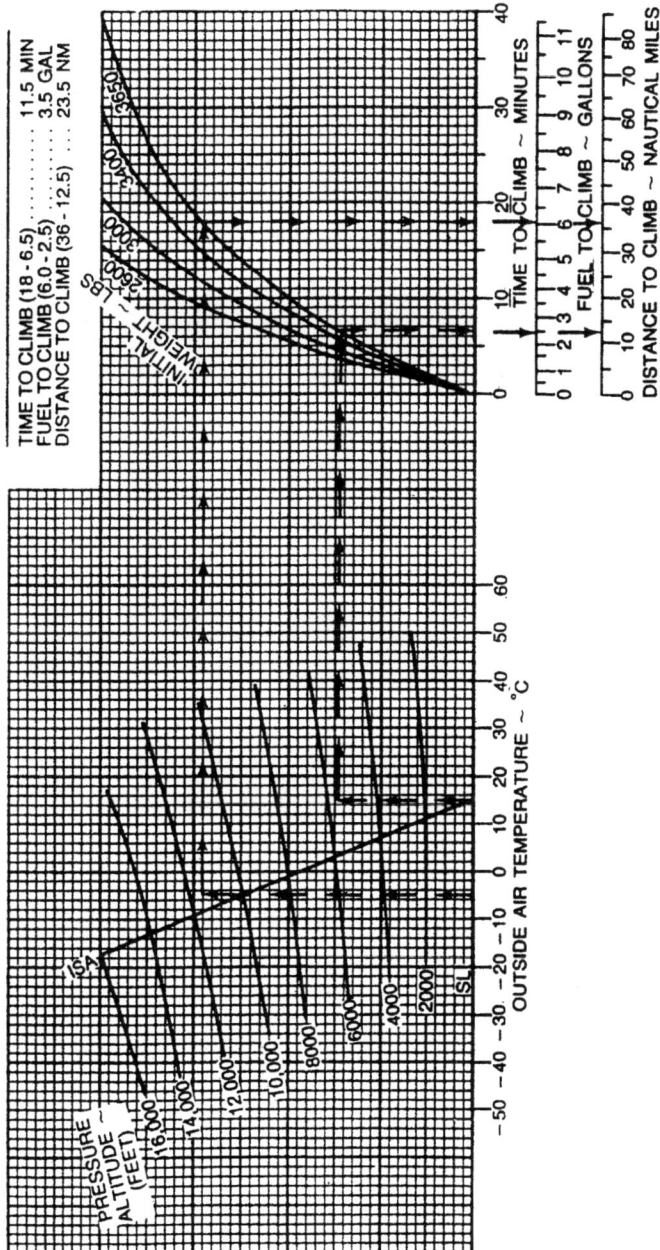

FLIGHT PLANNING & MONITORING   7

Figure 5.1

Example	
Aerodrome Pressure Altitude	3500'
Aerodrome OAT	+20°C
Cruising Pressure Altitude	13000'
OAT at 13000 ft	+01°C
TOW	3500 lb

Determine the time, fuel used and distance covered in the climb.

Solution

		Time (minutes)	Fuel (USG)	Still air distance (NM)
1.	Enter at the base at +01°C and go vertically to 13000 ft, then right to 3500 lb and vertically down to read, at the base	21.00	6.90	43.00
2.	Enter at the base at +20°C and go vertically to 3500 ft, then right to 3500 lb and vertically down to read, at the base	4.00	1.40	7.00
3.	Subtract line 2 from line 1	17.00	5.50	36.00

If a distance taking into account a wind component is required, for example a 25KT headwind, this must be factored by (GS/TAS) as follows:

Take the mean pressure altitude:

$$\frac{13\,000 + 3\,500 \text{ ft}}{2} = 8\,250'$$

and OAT for the climb:

$$\frac{01 + 20 \text{ °C}}{2} = +10\tfrac{1}{2}°C$$

Use these to find TAS from the IAS stated on the graph (110 KT) using the CRP-5:

Mean climb TAS = 127KT

Factor the still air distance:

$$36 \text{ NM} \times \frac{GS}{TAS}$$

$$= 36 \text{ NM} \times \frac{100}{125}$$

Wind factored distance = 28.34NM

Distance in the climb may alternatively be found by applying the w/v to the course and TAS to find heading and GS, then applying the climb time to the GS to find distance

An alternative method for approximating the TAS is to divide the still air distance (36 NM) by the time (17 min) and multiply by 60.

5.3   Cruise

At top of climb it is normal to reduce power and lean the mixture. This reduces the rate of fuel burn and reduces wear and tear on the engine

The actual cruise power setting is selected by consideration of speed, range and endurance. It will also be affected by the selection of power setting, RPM and altitude by environmental conditions, especially ambient temperature.

The higher the manifold pressure and RPM the higher the speed, but speed can only be increased at the expense of both range and endurance.

Use the Recommended Cruise Power Setting tables in the CAP 697 to extract required data for cruise engine settings.

5.4   Recommended Cruise Power Settings CAP 697 Fig 2.2 Table 2.2.1

Table 2.2.1

| 20°C LEAN |

25.0 IN. HG (or full throttle) @ 2500 RPM

Of Peak EGT   Cruise Lean Mixture
                                  3400 lbs.

	Press. Alt.	IOAT		Man. Press.	Fuel Flow		Air Speed	
	Feet	°C	°F	IN. HG	PPH	GPH	KIAS	KTAS
ISA −20°C (ISA −36°F)	0	-3	27	25.0	86.3	14.4	168	159
	2000	-6	20	25.0	89.3	14.9	168	164
	4000	-10	13	25.0	92.3	15.4	168	169
	6000	-14	6	24.1	89.8	15.0	164	170
	8000	-18	-1	22.3	82.6	13.8	157	168
	10,000	-22	-8	20.6	76.0	12.7	150	165
	12,000	-26	-15	19.1	70.2	11.7	143	162
	14,000	-30	-23	17.7	65.5	10.9	135	158
	16,000	-35	-30	16.3	60.8	10.1	126	152
Standard Day (ISA)	0	17	63	25.0	82.9	13.8	163	160
	2000	14	56	25.0	85.6	14.3	163	165
	4000	10	50	25.0	88.5	14.8	163	170
	6000	6	42	24.1	86.1	14.4	159	171
	8000	2	35	22.3	79.3	13.2	152	169
	10,000	-2	28	20.6	73.3	12.2	145	166
	12,000	-6	21	19.1	67.8	11.3	137	162
	14,000	-10	13	17.7	63.5	10.6	129	157
	16,000	-15	6	16.3	59.1	9.9	120	150
ISA + 20°C (ISA + 36°F)	0	37	99	25.0	79.5	13.3	158	161
	2000	34	92	25.0	82.1	13.7	158	166
	4000	30	86	25.0	84.7	14.1	158	171
	6000	26	79	24.1	82.5	13.8	154	172
	8000	22	71	22.3	76.2	12.7	147	169
	10,000	18	64	20.6	70.5	11.8	140	165
	12,000	14	57	19.1	65.5	10.9	132	161
	14,000	10	49	17.7	61.5	10.3	123	155
	16,000	5	42	16.3	57.5	9.6	113	146

Notes: 1.   Full throttle manifold pressure settings are approximate
       2.   Shaded area represents operation with full throttle
       3.   Fuel flows are to be used for flight planning only and will vary from
             aeroplane to aeroplane. Lean using the EGT.

FLIGHT PLANNING & MONITORING   8

Figure 5.2

5.5 Recommended Cruise Power Settings CAP 697 Fig 2.2 Table 2.2.3

TABLE   2.2.3

20°C LEAN

Of Peak EGT

23.0 IN. HG (OR FULL THROTTLE) @ 2300 RPM

CRUISE LEAN MIXTURE
3400 lbs.

	Press. Alt.	IOAT		Man. Press.	Fuel Flow		Air Speed	
	Feet	°C	°F	IN. HG.	PPH	GPH	KIAS	KTAS
ISA –20° C (ISA –36° F)	0	-3	26	23.0	67.6	11.3	152	144
	2000	-7	20	23.0	69.7	11.6	152	149
	4000	-11	13	23.0	72.1	12.0	153	154
	6000	-15	6	23.0	74.4	12.4	153	158
	8000	+18	-1	22.4	73.8	12.3	150	160
	10,000	-23	-9	20.7	68.4	11.4	143	157
	12,000	-17	-16	19.2	63.8	10.6	135	153
	14,000	-31	-23	17.8	60.0	10.0	127	148
	16,000	-35	-31	16.4	56.3	9.4	117	
Standard Day (ISA)	0	17	62	23.0	65.4	10.9	147	145
	2000	13	56	23.0	67.4	11.2	147	149
	4000	9	49	23.0	69.4	11.6	148	154
	6000	5	42	23.0	71.7	12.0	148	159
	8000	2	35	22.4	71.1	11.9	145	160
	10,000	-3	27	20.7	66.2	11.0	137	157
	12,000	-7	20	19.2	61.8	10.3	129	152
	14,000	-11	13	17.8	58.5	9.8	120	146
	16,000	-15	5	16.4	55.3	9.2	109	137
ISA + 20° C (ISA + 36° F)	0	37	98	23.0	63.2	10.5	142	145
	2000	33	92	23.0	65.1	10.9	143	149
	4000	29	85	23.0	67.1	11.2	143	154
	6000	25	78	23.0	69.0	11.5	142	158
	8000	22	71	22.4	68.5	11.4	140	160
	10,000	17	63	20.7	64.0	10.7	132	156
	12,000	13	56	19.2	60.0	10.0	123	151
	14,000	9	48	17.8	57.1	9.5	113	142
	16,000	•	•	•	•	•	•	•

NOTES:
1. Full throttle manifold pressure settings are approximate.
2. Shaded area represents operation with full throttle.
3. Fuel flows are to be used for flight planning only and will vary from aeroplane to aeroplane. Lean using the EGT.

Figure 5.3

CRANFIELD AVIATION TRAINING SCHOOL LTD. PART-FCL ATO N° 276
CATS INNOVATION CENTRE, LUTON, Bedfordshire LU2 8DL U.K.

www.catsaviation.com

5-6

Flight Planning & Monitoring

5.6 Economy Cruise Power Settings CAP 697 Fig 2.3 Table 2.3.1

TABLE   2.3.1

| 20°C LEAN |

21.0 IN. HG. (OR FULL THROTTLE) @ 2100 RPM

Of Peak EGT

CRUISE LEAN MIXTURE
3400 lbs.

	Press. Alt.	IOAT		Man. Press.	Fuel Flow		Air Speed	
	Feet	°C	°F	IN. HG.	PPH	GPH	KIAS	KTAS
ISA – 20° C (ISA – 36°F)	0	-4	25	21.0	52.7	8.8	126	120
	2000	-8	18	21.0	54.0	9.0	128	125
	4000	-11	12	21.0	55.4	9.2	130	130
	6000	-15	5	21.0	56.9	9.5	131	136
	8000	-19	-2	21.0	58.9	9.8	132	141
	10,000	-23	-9	20.8	60.1	10.0	132	144
	12,000	-27	-17	19.3	56.7	9.5	123	139
	14,000	-31	-24	17.9	54.5	9.1	113	132
	16,000	-35	-32	16.5	52.2	8.7	95	114
Standard Day (ISA)	0	16	61	21.0	51.8	8.6	120	118
	2000	12	54	21.0	53.1	8.9	123	124
	4000	9	48	21.0	54.4	9.1	124	129
	6000	5	41	21.0	55.7	9.3	125	134
	8000	1	34	21.0	57.3	9.6	126	140
	10,000	-3	27	20.8	58.5	9.8	126	143
	12,000	-7	19	19.3	55.6	9.3	116	137
	14,000	-11	12	17.9	53.5	8.9	103	125
	16,000	-	-	-	-	-	-	-
ISA + 20° C (ISA + 36°F)	0	36	97	21.0	50.8	8.5	114	115
	2000	32	90	21.0	52.1	8.7	116	121
	4000	29	83	21.0	53.4	8.9	118	127
	6000	25	77	21.0	54.7	9.1	119	132
	8000	21	70	21.0	55.9	9.3	120	137
	10,000	17	63	20.8	56.8	9.5	119	141
	12,000	13	55	19.3	54.5	9.1	108	131
	14,000	-	-	-	-	-	-	-
	16,000	-	-	-	-	-	-	-

NOTES:
1. Full throttle manifold pressure settings are approximate.
2. Shaded area represents operation with full throttle.
4. Fuel flows are to be used for flight planning only and will vary from aeroplane to aeroplane. Lean using the EGT.

Figure 5.4

5.7 Example

While the manner of extracting the information is identical for the three tables, it is interesting to compare the outputs.

For a 750 NM cruise in ISA at 5000':

25 IN HG 2500 RPM				23 IN HG 2300 RPM				21 IN HG 2100 RPM			
PPH	KIAS	KTAS	SAR*	PPH	KIAS	KTAS	SAR*	PPH	KIAS	KTAS	SAR*
87.3	161	170	1.945	70.55	148	156	2.215	55.05	124	131	2.383
Still air time 4 h 25 min				Still air time 4 h 48 min				Still air time 5 h 43 min			
Cruise fuel 385.6 lb				Cruise fuel 338.6 lb				Cruise fuel 314.7 lb			

*SAR = Specific range in still air

CRANFIELD AVIATION TRAINING SCHOOL LTD. PART-FCL ATO N° 276
CATS INNOVATION CENTRE, LUTON, Bedfordshire LU2 8DL U.K.

www.catsaviation.com

5-7

Flight Planning & Monitoring

SAR is the nautical air miles (NAM) flown for each pound of fuel used:

$$\frac{750}{385.6} = 1.945$$

Analysis shows:

* Although 25 IN HG 2500 RPM gives the shortest flight time, it uses the most fuel.

* 23 IN 2300 RPM uses less fuel but more time

* At 21 IN 2100 RPM fuel consumption is minimised but at a cost: the flight time is 54 min longer than the next slowest

* W/V may be allowed for by applying it to TAS and course stage by stage, obtaining GS and heading. If a MEAN WIND COMPONENT is required for a complete route, the following method is suggested:

Example

Stage	TAS	WC	GS	Distance	Time	WC x T
A - B	153	+15	168	112	40	+600
B - C	161	+25	186	155	50	+1250
C - D	158	+22	180	129	43	+946
D - E	163	-13	150	95	38	-494.00
Totals					171	+2302

$$\frac{+2302}{171} = +13.46$$

The wind component (WC) is multiplied by the time in minutes for each stage. Totals are taken of time and 'WC x time'. The 'WC x time' total is then divided by the time total giving the MEAN WIND COMPONENT for all four stages where '+' signifies a tailwind and '-' a headwind.

+	tailwind
−	headwind

5.8 Range and endurance

For each power setting curve in Figure 2.4 the range initially decreases with altitude but then, at the level at which full throttle is reached, the range starts to increase again

At a given altitude, greater ranges are possible with lower power settings

This is a still air range and a head/tail wind component may significantly affect it. Values of TAS are given at various levels on each range/power setting curve

5.9   *CAP697 Fig 2.4 Range Profile*

Figure 2.4   RANGE

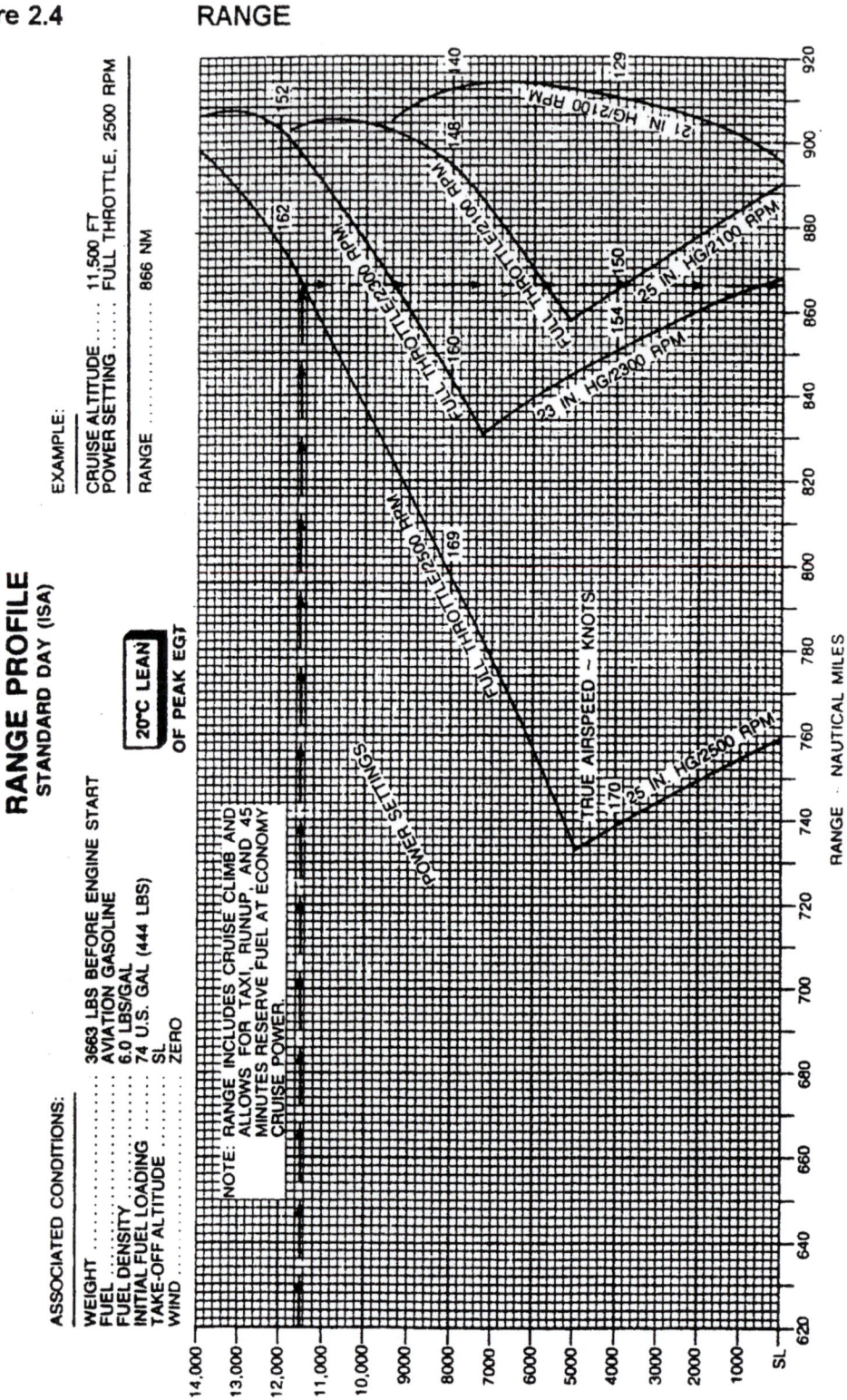

Figure 5.5

CRANFIELD AVIATION TRAINING SCHOOL LTD. PART-FCL ATO N° 276
CATS INNOVATION CENTRE, LUTON, Bedfordshire LU2 8DL U.K.

www.catsaviation.com

The worked example shows that, at an altitude of 11500 ft with power setting at full throttle at 2500 RPM, the still air range is 866 NM.

Further examples
What is the still air range for the aeroplane if operated at full throttle at 2300 RPM at an altitude of 8000 ft? (845 NAM)

At what altitude could a range of 890 NAM be achieved with full throttle at 2300 RPM 23 Hg? (11000 ft)

What is the maximum range (NAM) that could be achieved with full throttle at 2100 RPM and at what altitude? (905 NAM, 10800 ft)

Endurance is the amount of airborne time possible for the fuel carried

5.10 CAP697 Fig 2.5 Endurance Profile

Figure 2.5   ENDURANCE

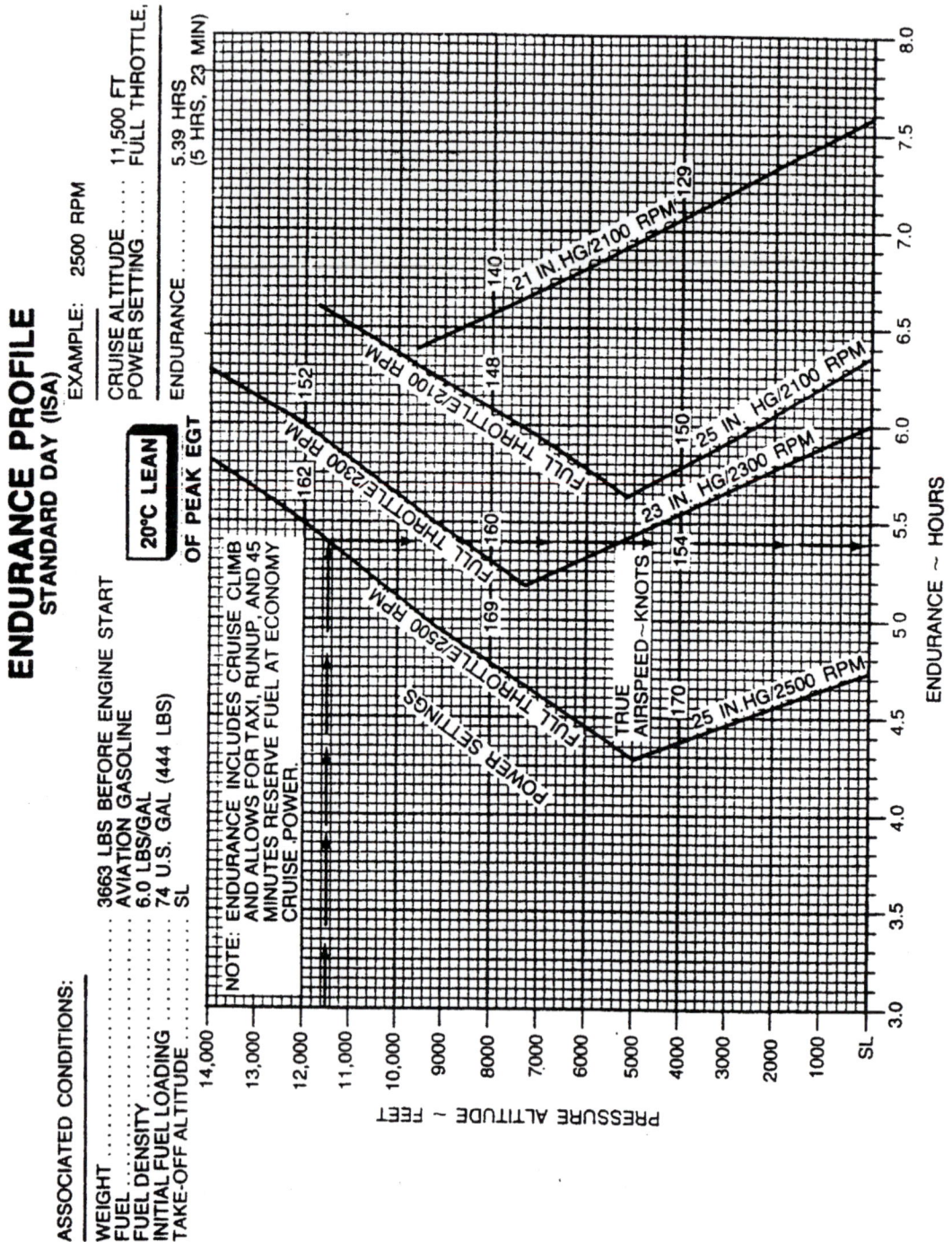

Figure 5.6

The worked example shows that at 2500 RPM and power set to full throttle, an endurance of 5.39 hours is available.

![CATS logo] **CRANFIELD AVIATION TRAINING SCHOOL LTD.** PART-FCL ATO N° 276
CATS INNOVATION CENTRE, LUTON, Bedfordshire LU2 8DL U.K.   www.catsaviation.com

5-11   Flight Planning & Monitoring

Further examples

What is the endurance available with power set to full throttle 2300 RPM at an altitude of 10000 ft? (5.65 hours)

What is the % increase in endurance when flying at an altitude of 8000 ft at 2100 RPM if power is set to 21.00 inches Hg instead of full throttle? (7.38 %)

Using Figure 1.2 what is the % increase in range made possible with the above % increase in endurance? (2.01%)

5.11 Completing a fuel plan

Route plans show for each sector the distance, course and forecast w/v. For example a flight is to be conducted at 8000 ft at full throttle with 2300 RPM. Temperatures throughout are ISA. Departure aerodrome is at MSL. Take off mass 3600 lb.

Establish the total fuel required assuming:
- 12 lb of fuel are required for start-up, engine test and taxiing
- Fuel for take off and climb
- Fuel for cruise to overhead destination
- An allowance of 10 lb for circuit, landing and taxi
- Sufficient for 45 minutes holding at 21.00 IN HG. 2100 RPM at 2000 ft
- A contingency reserve of 10% of (3) above

Solution

Fuel Summary		Trip fuel 27.00 USG
	Take off	12 lb
	Trip fuel	162 lb
	Circuit	10 lb
	Holding	40 lb
	Contingency	16 lb
	Total Fuel	240 lb

Example

Find the time, fuel used and distance covered in a 25 kt tailwind in the climb from an aerodrome at pressure altitude 1500 ft, OAT +15°C to an initial cruising level of 14000 ft (OAT -15°C) if the TOW is 3650 lb

CRANFIELD AVIATION TRAINING SCHOOL LTD. PART-FCL ATO N° 276
CATS INNOVATION CENTRE, LUTON, Bedfordshire LU2 8DL U.K.

www.catsaviation.com

5-12

Flight Planning & Monitoring

Solution

		Time (minutes)	Fuel (USG)	Still air distance (NM)
1.	Enter at the base at -15°C and go vertically to 14000 ft, then right to 3650 lb and vertically down to read, at the base	24.5	7.7	50
2.	Enter at the base at +15°C and go vertically to 1500 ft, then right to 3650 lb and vertically down to read, at the base	1.5	0.6	3
3.	Subtract line 2 from line 1	23	7.1	47

Approximate TAS:

$$\frac{47}{23} \times 60 = 123 \text{ kt}$$

Factor distance by

$$\frac{GS}{TAS} \times \text{Still air distance}$$

Gives:

$$\frac{(123 + 25)}{123} \times 47 = 56.55 \text{ NM in wind}$$

Example

Cruising at 14000 ft at OAT -15°C, what will be the fuel and time for a cruise of 600 NM in a 30 KT headwind if cruise power setting 25.0 IN HG (or full throttle) at 2500 RPM is selected?

Solution

At 14000 ft OAT in ISA is -13°C, so since the actual OAT is -15°C (ISA - 02°C) the ISA block is used WITHOUT INTERPOLATION

From CAP697 Figure 2.2.1:
- Full throttle boost (17.7 IN HG)
- Fuel flow (63.5 PPH)
- IAS (129 KT)
- TAS (157 KT)

TAS 157 KT, wind component -30 KT, GS 127 KT

600 NM at GS 127 KT takes 4 hours 43½ min. Figure 2.5 shows that this is within the endurance
4 hours 43½ min at fuel flow 63.5 PPH gives fuel required 300 lb

Example

Find the still air range and endurance at pressure altitude 10000' if cruise power setting 25.0 IN HG (or full throttle) at 2100 RPM is used

Solution

Range (Figure 2.4) 904 NM
Endurance (Figure 2.5) 6.38 h

CRANFIELD AVIATION TRAINING SCHOOL LTD. PART-FCL ATO N° 276
CATS INNOVATION CENTRE, LUTON, Bedfordshire LU2 8DL U.K.

www.catsaviation.com

5-13

Flight Planning & Monitoring

Self Assessment Test 05

1   (For this question use the Flight Planning Manual SEP 1 Figure 2.5)
     Given:
     FL 75
     Lean mixture
     Full throttle
     2300 RPM
     Take-off fuel: 444 lbs
     Take-off from MSL
     Find: Endurance in hours.
A)   05:20
B)   04:42
C)   05:23
D)   05:12

2   (For this question use annex 033-4736A or Flight Planning Manual SEP 1 Table 2.2.3)
     Given:
     FL 75
     OAT +10°C
     Lean mixture
     2300 RPM
     Find:
     Fuel flow in gallons per hour (GPH) and TAS.
A)   11.6 GPH TAS: 143 kt
B)   71.1 GPH TAS: 143 kt
C)   68.5 GPH TAS: 160 kt
D)   11.6 GPHTAS: 160 kt

3   (For this question use the Flight Planning Manual SEP 1 Figure 2.1)
     Given:
     FL 75
     OAT: +5°C
     During climb: average head wind component 20 kt
     Take-off from MSL with the initial mass of 3 650 lbs.
     Find:
     Time and fuel to climb.
A)   9 min. 3,3 USG
B)   10 min. 3,6 USG
C)   7 min. 2,6 USG
D)   9 min. 2,7 USG

4   (For this question use the Flight Planning Manual SEP 1 Figure 2.1)
     Given:
     FL 75
     OAT: +5°C
     During climb: average head wind component 20 kt
     Take-off from MSL with the initial mass of 3 650 lbs.
     Find:
     Still air distance (NAM) and ground distance (NM) using the graph "time, fuel, distance to climb".

A)   14 NAM. 18 NM
B)   18 NAM.15 NM
C)   16 NAM.18 NM
D)   18 NAM. 13 NM

5   (For this question the Flight Planning Manual SEP 1 Figure 2.1)
     Given: Take-off mass 3500 lbs, departure aerodrome pressure altitude 2500 ft,
     OAT +10°C,
              First cruising level: FL 140, OAT -5°C
     Find the time, fuel and still air distance to climb.

A)   23 min, 7.7 GAL, 50 NAM
B)   22 min, 6.7 GAL, 45 NAM
C)   24 min, 7.7 GAL, 47 NAM
D)   16.5 min, 4.9 GAL, 34.5 NAM

6   (For this question use the Flight Planning Manual SEP 1 Figure 2.4)
     Given: Aeroplane mass at start-up 3663 lbs, Aviation gasoline (density 6 lbs/gal)-fuel load 74 gal, Take-off altitude sea level, Headwind 40 kt, Cruising altitude 8000 ft, Power setting full throttle 2300 RPM 20°C lean of peak EGT
     Calculate the range.

A)   547.5 NM
B)   633 NM
C)   844 NM
D)   730 NM

7   (For this question use the Flight Planning Manual SEP1 Figure 2.2 Table 2.2.2)
     A flight has to be made with the single engine sample aeroplane. For the fuel calculation allow 10 lbs fuel for start up and taxi, 3 minutes and 1 gallon of additional fuel to allow for the climb, 10 minutes and no fuel correction for the descent.
     Planned flight time (overhead to overhead) is 03 hours and 12 minutes.
     Reserve fuel 30% of the trip fuel.
     Power setting is 25 in.HG (or full throttle), 2100 RPM, 20°C lean.
     Flight level is 70 and the OAT 11°C.
     The minimum block fuel is:

A)   283 lbs
B)   268 lbs
C)   252 lbs
D)   215 lbs

CRANFIELD AVIATION TRAINING SCHOOL LTD. PART-FCL ATO N° 276
CATS INNOVATION CENTRE, LUTON, Bedfordshire LU2 8DL U.K.   www.catsaviation.com

5-15   Flight Planning & Monitoring

8   (For this question use the Flight Planning Manual SEP1 Figure 2.2 Table 2.2.3)
    A flight has to be made with the single engine sample aeroplane. For the fuel calculation allow 10 lbs
    fuel for start up and taxi, 3 minutes and 1 gallon of additional fuel to allow for the climb, 10 minutes and
    no fuel correction for the descent.
    Planned flight time (overhead to overhead) is 02 hours and 37 minutes.
    Reserve fuel 30% of the trip fuel.
    Power setting is 23 in.HG (or full throttle), 2300 RPM, 20°C lean.
    Flight level is 50 and the OAT -5°C.
    The minimum block fuel is:
A)   208 lbs
B)   270 lbs
C)   250 lbs
D)   265 lbs

Self Assessment Test 05 Answers

1	D
2	D
3	A
4	B
5	B
6	B
7	A
8	D

CRANFIELD AVIATION TRAINING SCHOOL LTD. PART-FCL ATO N° 276
CATS INNOVATION CENTRE, LUTON, Bedfordshire LU2 8DL U.K.

www.catsaviation.com

5-17

Flight Planning & Monitoring

CHAPTER 6

Fuel planning for a Multi-Engine Piston (MEP) aeroplane

6.1   Climb

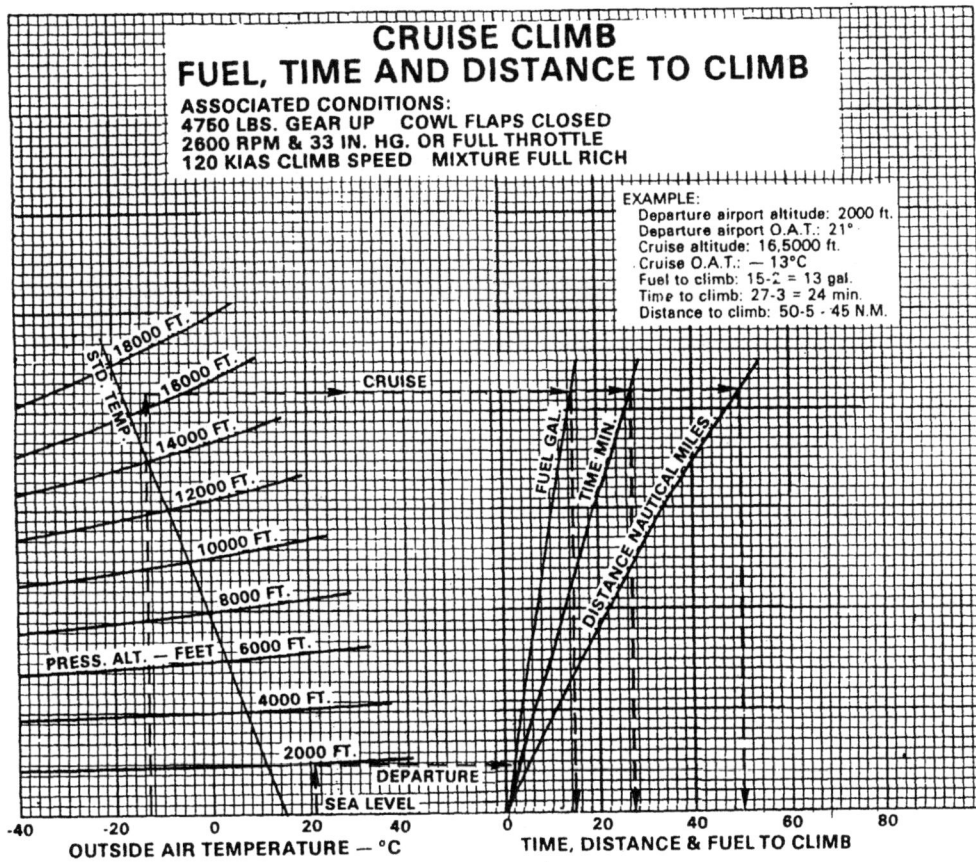

Figure 6.1 Cruise climb fuel, time and distance to climb (CAP 697 Figure 3.1)

Using CAP 697 Figure 3.1 example:

1.   Enter Figure 3.1 with the elevation of the departure airfield and its temperature. From this intersection, move horizontally so as to draw a line through the fuel, time and distance curves.

Note the values of each:

Fuel 2 gal
Time 3 min
Distance 5 NM

2.   Now enter the graph with the temperature at the cruise level and move vertically to the cruise altitude. From this intersection move horizontally to draw a line through the fuel, time and distance curves.

Note the values of each:

Fuel 15 gall
Time 27 min
Distance 50 NM

Then, subtract (1) from (2) to obtain the fuel time and distance to take off and climb to the cruise altitude;

Fuel 15 – 2 = 13 gallons
Time 27 – 3 = 24 minutes
Distance 50 – 5 = 45 NM

6.2 Cruise

6.2.1 Range data

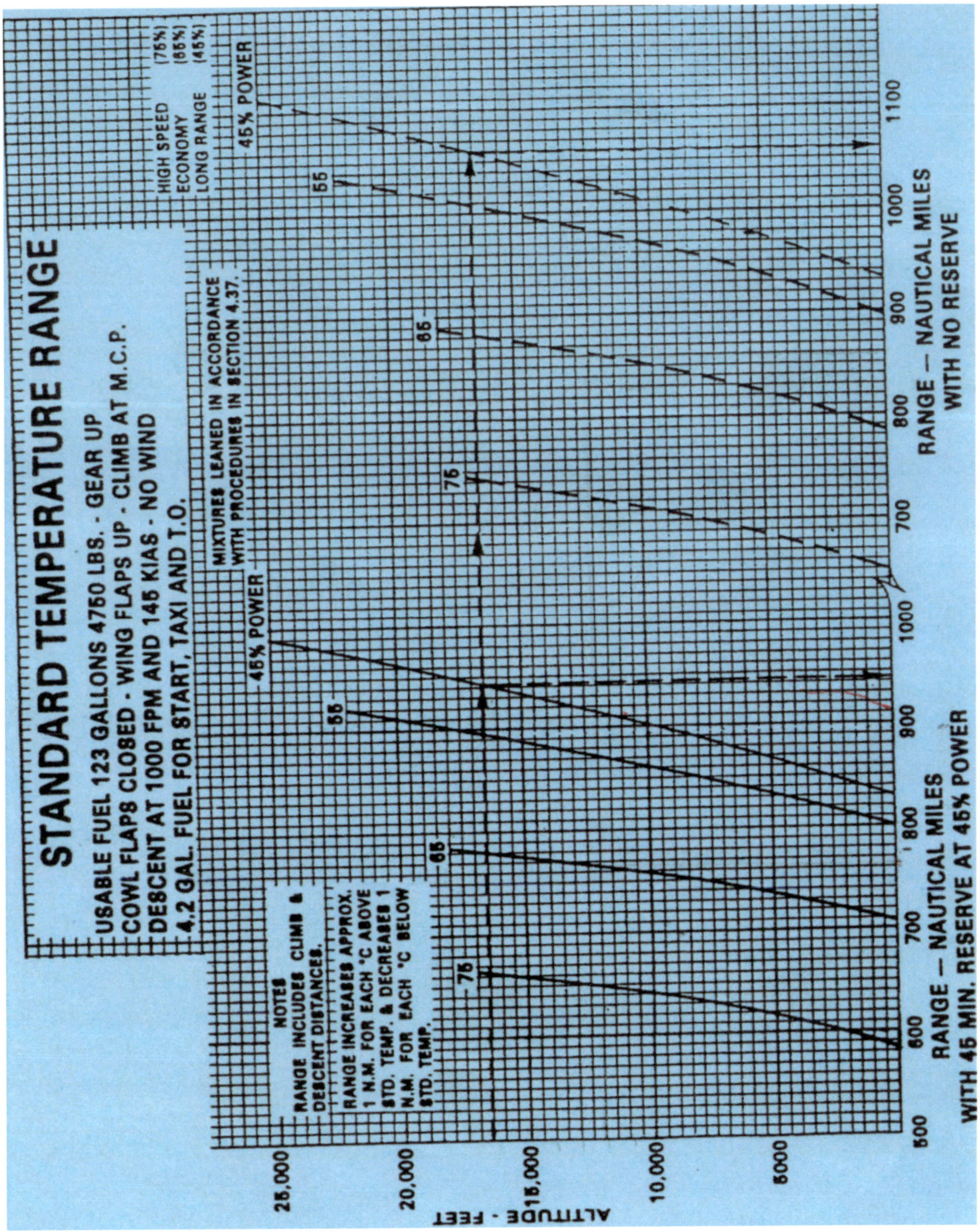

Figure 6.2

Figure 6.2 presents range data. The graph is a double presentation in that one notes that there are two distance scales at the base of range with a 45 min reserve at 45% power and with no reserve.

CRANFIELD AVIATION TRAINING SCHOOL LTD. PART-FCL ATO N° 276
CATS INNOVATION CENTRE, LUTON, Bedfordshire LU2 8DL U.K.

www.catsaviation.com

6-3

Flight Planning & Monitoring

Example

Find the still air range of the aeroplane at 12500 ft at all power settings, with and without a 45 min reserve at 45% power

Solution

Take a horizontal line through the graph, entering at the left at (pressure) altitude 12500 ft. At the relevant labelled lines drop vertically to read the ranges:

Power	45 minute reserve (45% power)	Without reserve
45%	918 NM	1030 NM
55%	875 NM	985 NM
65%	768 NM	865 NM
75%	650 NM	725 NM

CRANFIELD AVIATION TRAINING SCHOOL LTD. PART-FCL ATO N° 276
CATS INNOVATION CENTRE, LUTON, Bedfordshire LU2 8DL U.K.

www.catsaviation.com

6-4

Flight Planning & Monitoring

6.2.2 Selecting cruise power

The four percentage power columns in CAP 697 Figure 3.3 allow selection of high speed, economy or long range. Each percentage power column is subdivided to allow the selection of the desired RPM and manifold pressure against altitude in a standard atmosphere.

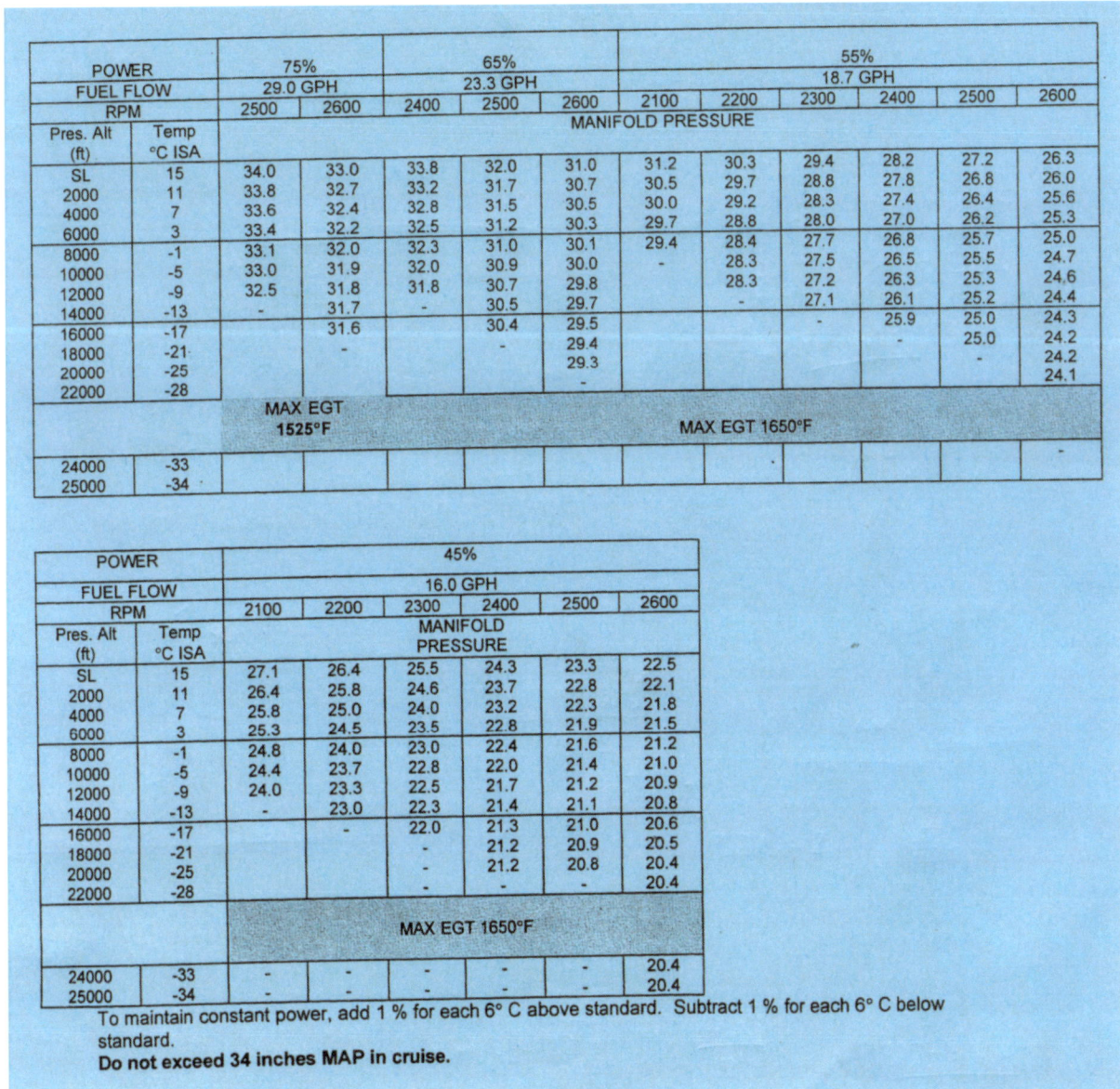

POWER		75%		65%			55%				
FUEL FLOW		29.0 GPH		23.3 GPH			18.7 GPH				
RPM		2500	2600	2400	2500	2600	2100	2200	2300	2400	2500	2600
Pres. Alt (ft)	Temp °C ISA	MANIFOLD PRESSURE									
SL	15	34.0	33.0	33.8	32.0	31.0	31.2	30.3	29.4	28.2	27.2	26.3
2000	11	33.8	32.7	33.2	31.7	30.7	30.5	29.7	28.8	27.8	26.8	26.0
4000	7	33.6	32.4	32.8	31.5	30.5	30.0	29.2	28.3	27.4	26.4	25.6
6000	3	33.4	32.2	32.5	31.2	30.3	29.7	28.8	28.0	27.0	26.2	25.3
8000	-1	33.1	32.0	32.3	31.0	30.1	29.4	28.4	27.7	26.8	25.7	25.0
10000	-5	33.0	31.9	32.0	30.9	30.0	-	28.3	27.5	26.5	25.5	24.7
12000	-9	32.5	31.8	31.8	30.7	29.8		28.3	27.2	26.3	25.3	24.6
14000	-13	-	31.7	-	30.5	29.7		-	27.1	26.1	25.2	24.4
16000	-17		31.6		30.4	29.5			-	25.9	25.0	24.3
18000	-21		-		-	29.4				-	25.0	24.2
20000	-25					29.3					-	24.2
22000	-28					-						24.1
		MAX EGT 1525°F		MAX EGT 1650°F								
24000	-33											-
25000	-34											

POWER		45%					
FUEL FLOW		16.0 GPH					
RPM		2100	2200	2300	2400	2500	2600
Pres. Alt (ft)	Temp °C ISA	MANIFOLD PRESSURE					
SL	15	27.1	26.4	25.5	24.3	23.3	22.5
2000	11	26.4	25.8	24.6	23.7	22.8	22.1
4000	7	25.8	25.0	24.0	23.2	22.3	21.8
6000	3	25.3	24.5	23.5	22.8	21.9	21.5
8000	-1	24.8	24.0	23.0	22.4	21.6	21.2
10000	-5	24.4	23.7	22.8	22.0	21.4	21.0
12000	-9	24.0	23.3	22.5	21.7	21.2	20.9
14000	-13	-	23.0	22.3	21.4	21.1	20.8
16000	-17		-	22.0	21.3	21.0	20.6
18000	-21			-	21.2	20.9	20.5
20000	-25			-	21.2	20.8	20.4
22000	-28			-	-	-	20.4
		MAX EGT 1650°F					
24000	-33	-	-	-	-	-	20.4
25000	-34	-	-	-	-	-	20.4

To maintain constant power, add 1 % for each 6° C above standard. Subtract 1 % for each 6° C below standard.
Do not exceed 34 inches MAP in cruise.

Figure 6.3

CRANFIELD AVIATION TRAINING SCHOOL LTD. PART-FCL ATO N° 276
CATS INNOVATION CENTRE, LUTON, Bedfordshire LU2 8DL U.K.

www.catsaviation.com

6-5

Flight Planning & Monitoring

6.2.3 *Endurance data*

Example

Find the Endurance of the aeroplane at 12500 ft at all power settings, with and without a 45 min reserve at 45% power.

Solution

Take a horizontal line through Figure 2.3 entering at the left at (pressure) altitude 12500 ft. At the relevant labelled lines drop vertically to read endurance for each condition.

Power	45 min reserve (45% power)	Without reserve*
45%	6.33 hours	7.08 hours
55%	5.46 hours	6.1 hours
65%	4.43 hours	5 hours
75%	3.6 hours	4.1 hours

*'Without reserve' exceeds 'with reserve' by 45 min only in the 45% power case, since in the other cases the power is maintained above 45% during the 'reserve time'

CRANFIELD AVIATION TRAINING SCHOOL LTD. PART-FCL ATO N° 276
CATS INNOVATION CENTRE, LUTON, Bedfordshire LU2 8DL U.K.

www.catsaviation.com

6-6

Flight Planning & Monitoring

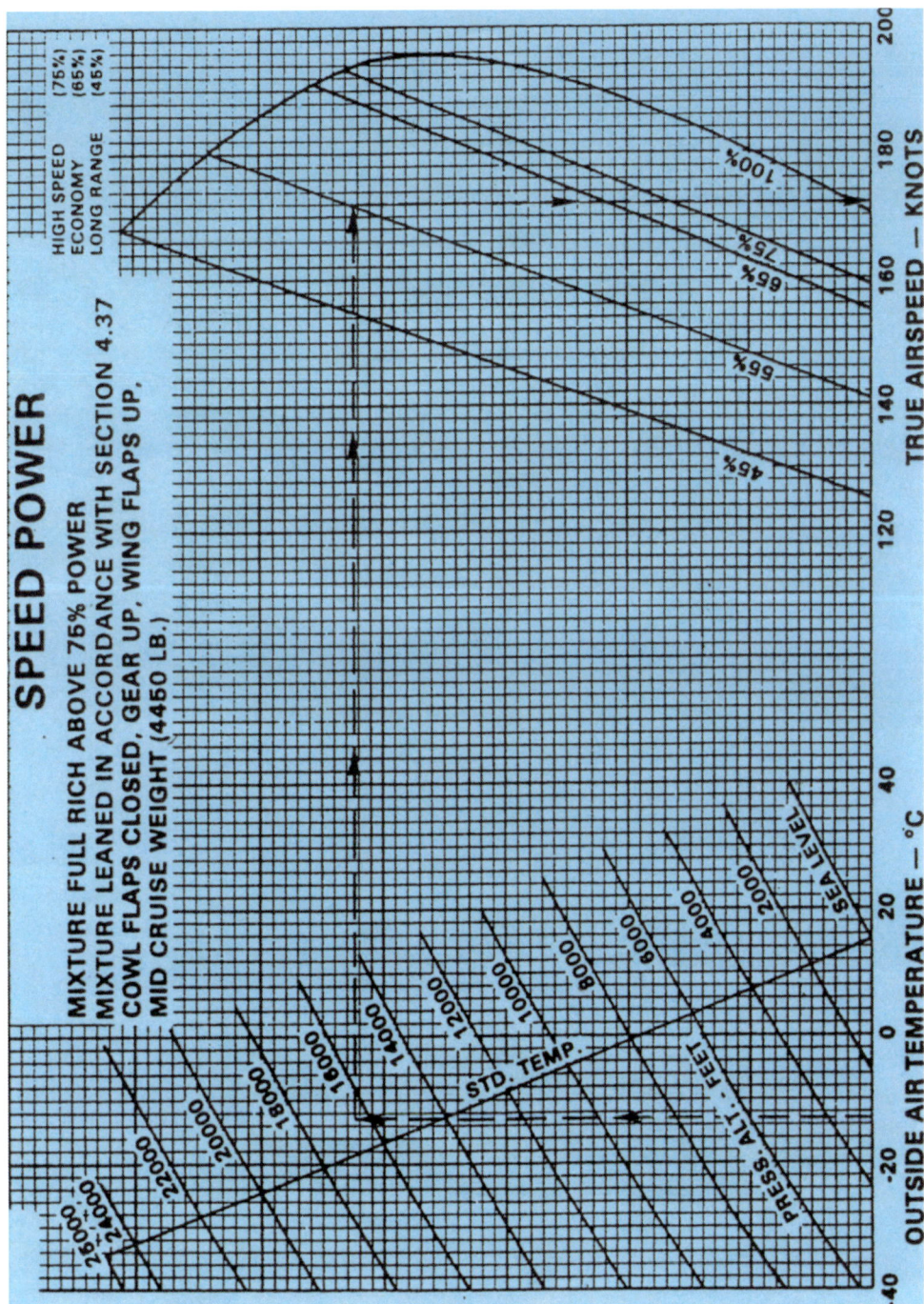

Figure 6.4

Example

A flight is to be made at 10 000 ft (OAT -10°C) in MINIMUM TIME over 600 NM. What is the appropriate power setting, fuel flow and TAS?

Solution

From CAP 697 Figure 3.3 select the section for the highest power setting, which is 75%.

There is a choice between 2500 RPM and 2600 RPM, with manifold pressures (MAP) given for both. Inspection of the figures at 10 000 ft shows that at the LOWER RPM (preferred) MAP 34 IN HG will not be exceeded.

CRANFIELD AVIATION TRAINING SCHOOL LTD. PART-FCL ATO N° 276
CATS INNOVATION CENTRE, LUTON, Bedfordshire LU2 8DL U.K.   www.catsaviation.com

6-7   Flight Planning & Monitoring

From the table:

Fuel flow = 29.0 GPH (174 PPH)
MAP (2500 RPM) = 33.0 IN HG
OAT in ISA = -05°C

Since the ACTUAL OAT is -10°C (ISA - 05°C) a correction of -1% is appropriate, giving:

Fuel Flow = 28.7 GPH (172 PPH)
MAP (2500 RPM) = 32.7 IN HG

At figure 2.4 enter at bottom left at OAT -10°C and go vertically to 10 000 ft, then horizontally right to the line labelled 75%. Drop vertically to read TAS 178 kt.

6.2.4   *Descent*

For the single engine aeroplane descent was not considered since fuel required for the descent differed very little from that required for the same distance in a cruise configuration.

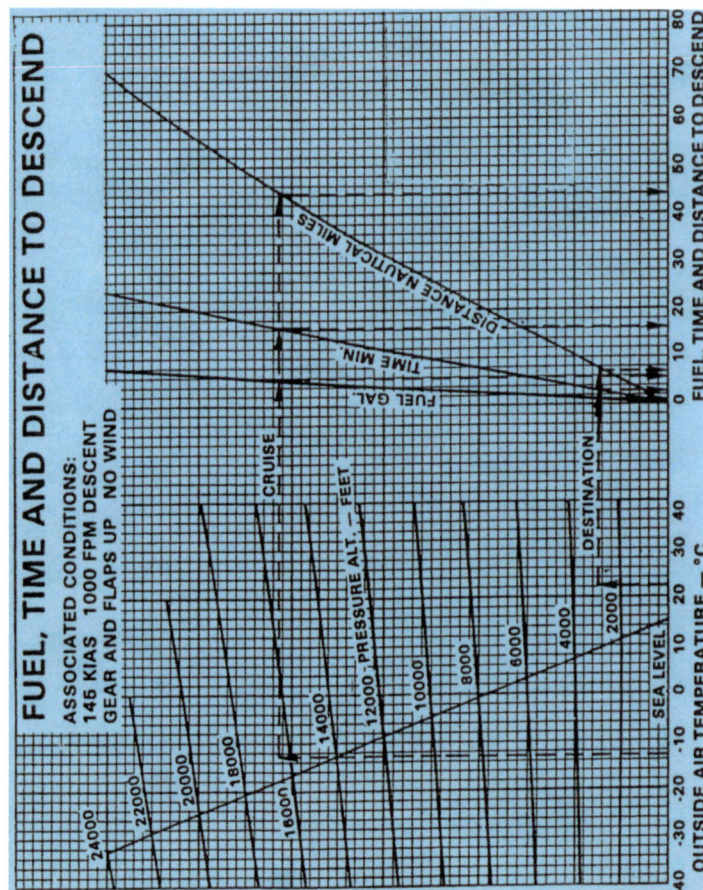

Given the higher power and higher fuel consumption of a twin engine aeroplane there is a significant difference and the descent is allowed for as a separate section of flight

6.2.5   In-flight fuel checks

In-flight fuel checks are required by Appendix 1 to JAR-OPS 1.375
These checks must be carried out at regular intervals and used to:
- Compare actual with planned consumption
- Ensure that the remaining fuel is sufficient to complete the flight
- Predict the fuel remaining at the destination

Methods of tabulating these checks vary.
A log, prepared before flight, to show expected fuel remaining at significant route points may be used so that actual may be compared. At the same time the fuel flow may be calculated by converting the amount of fuel used in unit time to an hourly rate and comparing the result with the planned fuel flow.
During the flight regular fuel checks are made. The results of these checks, that is, fuel remaining or fuel used, are then plotted on the graph and the situation, above, on or below the line, is immediately apparent.

It is common practice to allow a percentage of the fuel used from departure to destination (usually 5% to 7%) as a contingency allowance. This accounts for the actual conditions encountered enroute being less favourable than those forecast and used in the plan.

Alternate fuel is also required. Most presentations allow rapid assessment of the fuel requirement from destination to alternate (diversion fuel). Where no table is given the simplest method is to allow cruise fuel from destination to alternate.
45 min holding fuel is added as minimum reserve fuel, so block fuel comprises:
- Route fuel departure to destination
- Contingency fuel departure to destination
- Diversion or alternate fuel
- 45 minutes holding fuel
- Any further reserve at the discretion of the Captain

Self Assessment Test 06

1   (For this question use the Flight Planning Manual MEP1 Figure 3.1)
     A flight is to be made from one airport (elevation 3000 ft) to another in a multi engine piston aeroplane (MEP1). The cruising level will be FL 110. The temperature at FL 110 is ISA - 10° C. The temperature at the departure aerodrome is -1° C. Calculate the fuel to climb with mixture rich.
     A)   6 US gallon
     B)   9 US gallon
     C)   12 US gallon
     D)   3 US gallon

2   (For this question use the Flight Planning Manual MEP1 Figure 3.6)
     A flight is to be made to an airport, pressure altitude 3000 ft, in a multi engine piston aeroplane (MEP1). The forecast OAT for the airport is -1° C. The cruising level will be FL 110, where OAT is -10° C. Calculate the still air descent distance for:
     145 KIAS
     Rate of descent 1000 fpm
     Gears and flaps up
     A)   20 NM
     B)   29 NM
     C)   36 NM
     D)   25 NM

3   (For this question use the Flight Planning Manual MEP 1 Figure 3.2)
     A flight is to be made in a multi engine piston aeroplane (MEP1). The cruising level will be 11000ft. The outside air temperature at FL is -15 ° C. The usable fuel is 123 US gallons. The power is set to economic cruise. Find the range in NM with 45 min reserve fuel at 45 % power.
     A)   752 NM
     B)   852 NM
     C)   610 NM
     D)   602 NM

4   (For this question use the Flight Planning Manual MEP 1 Figure 3.3)
     A flight has to be made with a multi engine piston aeroplane (MEP 1). For the fuel calculations take 5 US gallons for the taxi, and an additional 13 minutes at cruise condition to account for climb and descent. Calculated time from overhead to overhead is 1h47min. Power setting is 45%, 2600 RPM. Calculated reserve fuel is 30% of the trip fuel. FL 100. Temperature -5°C. Find the minimum block fuel.
     A)   47 US gallons.
     B)   37 US gallons
     C)   60 US gallons
     D)   470 US gallons

CRANFIELD AVIATION TRAINING SCHOOL LTD. PART-FCL ATO N° 276
CATS INNOVATION CENTRE, LUTON, Bedfordshire LU2 8DL U.K.
CATS
www.catsaviation.com
6-10
Flight Planning & Monitoring

Self Assessment Test 06 Answers

1	A
2	A
3	A
4	A

CHAPTER 7
Fuel planning for a Medium Range Jet Transport (MRJT) aeroplane

7.1 Introduction

As the aeroplane mass and range capability increase so the range of fuel flows increases

Fuel flow is affected by:
- Mass
- Position of centre of gravity
- Cruise altitude
- Temperature

Excess fuel means that the aeroplane is heavier than necessary, causing fuel flow to increase and a fuel penalty. If fuel at destination is more expensive than at the departure point, this penalty may be outweighed by the fuel cost differential.

7.2 Optimum altitude

A jet aeroplane tries to be generally operated at the optimum available altitude to minimise fuel burn

It is normal for the performance manual to provide data for a selection of different cruise options:
- Long range cruise (LRC)
- Normal cruise
- High speed cruise

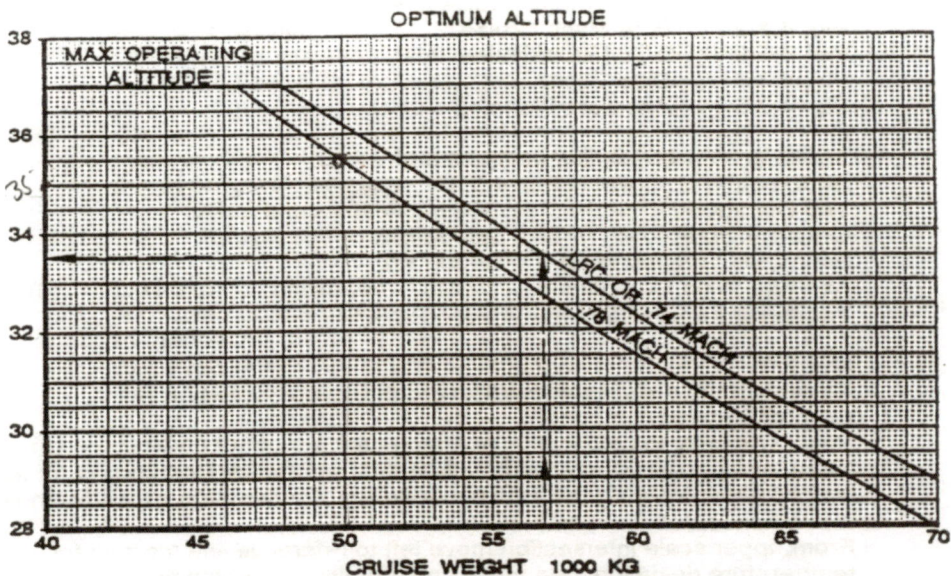

OPTIMUM ALTITUDE

Optimum altitude increases as the aeroplane mass decreases

Operating above optimum altitude reduces buffet boundaries while operating below it results in fuel penalties

7.3 Fuel penalties

As the cruise progresses and mass reduces due to fuel burn, altitude is progressively increased. Unfortunately, a cruise climb is not normally consistent with air traffic control requirements and as a compromise a step climb is used instead. In this procedure, the cruising altitude of the aeroplane is increased in 4000' steps so that it remains as close to the optimum altitude as possible.

If you are unable to cruise at your optimum altitude a fuel penalty will be incurred which may be calculated using the Fuel Mileage Penalty % table in CAP 697 on page 24.

Example: What fuel penalty may be incurred if an aeroplane with a Brake Release Weight of 60000 kg cruises at 29000' instead of optimum altitude?

Solution: First of all use CAP 697 Figure 4.2.1 to find optimum altitude.

Enter graph with brake release weight of 60000 kg

Move vertically to selected cruise profile eg. LRC

Move horizontally to read optimum altitude (32900')

Refer to the Fuel Mileage Penalty % table in CAP 697 on page 24

You are scheduled to cruise at 29000' which is 3900' OFF the Optimum Condition

The LRC Fuel Mileage Penalty % is 4%

7.4 Short distance cruise altitude

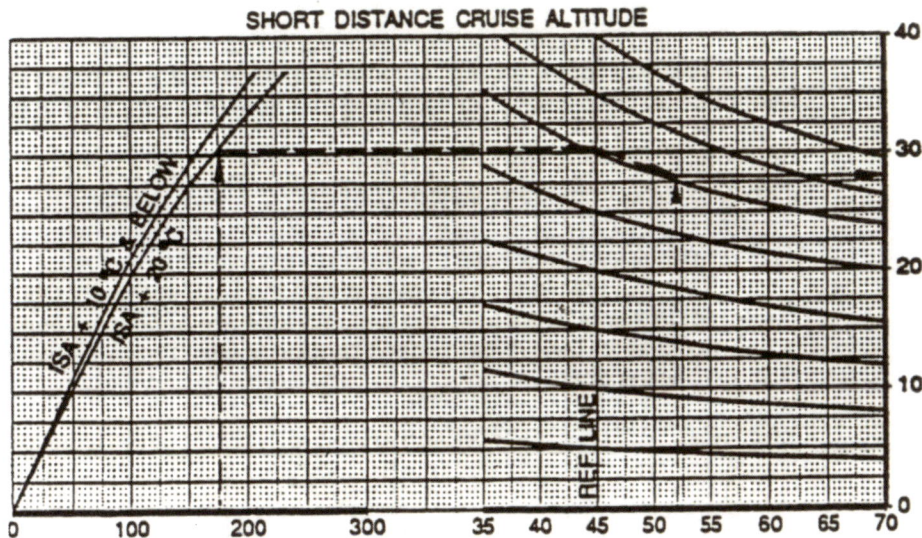

SHORT DISTANCE CRUISE ALTITUDE

At shorter distances between departure and destination the aeroplane may not be able to reach the optimum altitude before having to begin descent to be overhead the destination at the altitude for commencing final approach. In this case, it is still desirable to get as high as possible. Figure 4.3 shows a graph used to determine this 'short distance altitude'.

An example is overprinted at Fig 4.2.2 for:

Trip distance	175 NAM
Brake Release Weight (which we call TOM)	52 000 kg
Temperature	ISA + 20°C
Short distance cruise altitude	28000 ft

7.5   Simplified fuel planning

Performance manuals for most transport aeroplanes provide a rapid or simplified method of determining 'fuel required'.

Use of simplified fuel planning procedures generally implies acceptance of a small fuel penalty

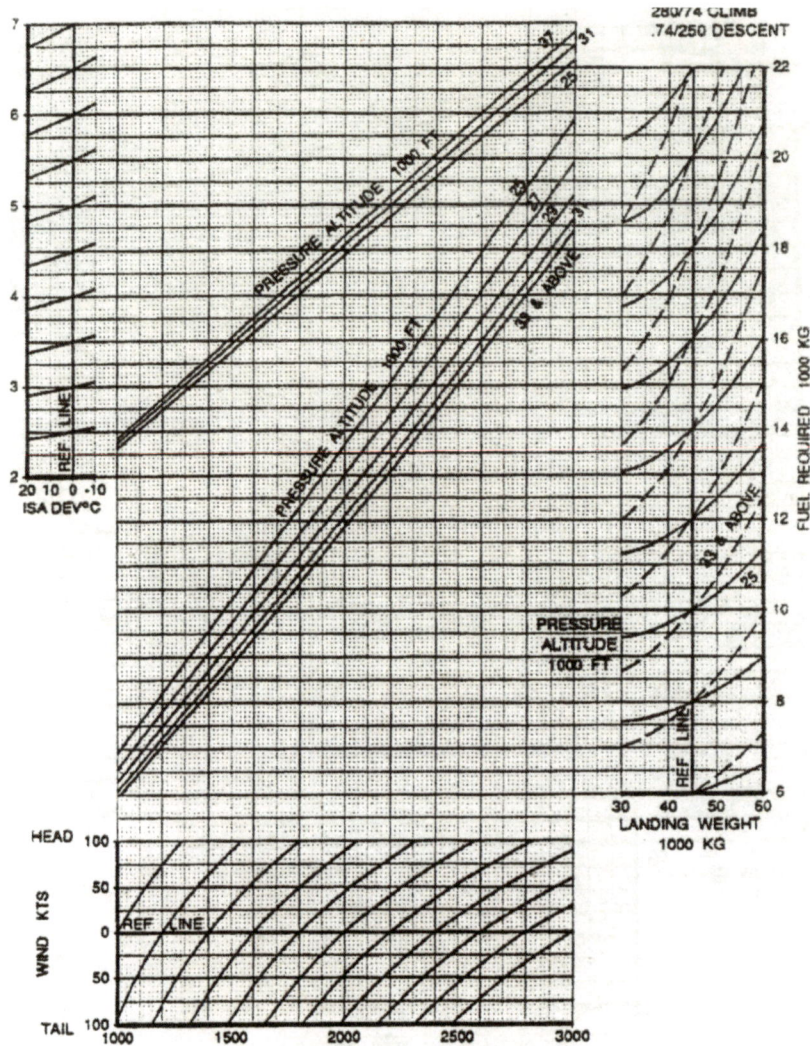

Example

Consider an aeroplane with take off mass 55 000 kg that is to operate a sector of 2 200 NM with an average headwind component of 30 KT.

Enter the graph at the base at 2 200 NM. Move vertically to intersect the wind reference line, follow the guidelines to the 30 KT headwind component. From this draw a vertical line to cut the two pressure altitude scales. From the intersection with cruising altitude on the lower scale (assume 33000 ft pressure altitude), determine the horizontal to the 'landing weight' reference line. The landing weight can be estimated by subtracting the fuel amount indicated at the right hand extension of the horizontal line (approximately 14 400 kg).This gives an approximate landing weight of 40 600 kg. From the intersection with the reference line follow the trade lines, interpolating between the dotted and solid if necessary. Here this is not necessary since altitude is above 23 000 ft therefore parallel the dashed lines to estimated landing weight. From the intersection with the vertical through landing mass draw a horizontal to the 'fuel required' scale and interpolate to obtain trip fuel 13 400 kg.

7.6 Fuel Planning

Data is provided in an aeroplane's performance manual that enables establishment of the fuel required. It is normal to provide this data in discrete sections:

- Climb
- Cruise options
- Descent
- Holding
- Diversion

7.7 Climb

Enter Figure 4.4 with cruise altitude and brake release weight (take off mass) and read time (minutes), fuel (kg), distance (NAM) and mean TAS (kt).

Convert NAM to Nautical Ground Miles (NGM) using the formula

$$NGM = \frac{NAM}{TAS} \times GS$$

Correct for airfield elevation.

Example
Assume:

- Optimum altitude for M0.74 cruise
- TOM 64 500 kg
- Temperature deviation 0 °C

Determine the climb fuel, time, distance and mean TAS

Solution
From Figure 4.1 determine optimum altitude 31200 ft

Determine the nearest suitable ATC cruising altitude:

Eastbound cruise levels are FL 290, 330, 370
Westbound cruise levels are FL 310, 350, 390

Assume flight is eastbound and use FL330 (for safety and fuel efficiency use the next level above). Remain at this level until the aeroplane mass has reduced. Enter table at FL330 to take off mass columns bracketing TOM 64 500 kg and interpolate:

TOM	Time	Fuel	Distance	TAS
66000	22	1850	129	385
64000	21	1700	119	383
~	1	150	10	2
64500	21.25	1740	121.5	383.5

7.8 Cruise

ISA +6°C TO +15°C

Press. Alt. Ft	Units Min/Kg. NAM/Kts	BRAKE RELEASE WEIGHT KG.										
		68000	66000	64000	62000	60000	58000	56000	52000	48000	44000	40000
37000	Time/Fuel				33/ 2350	27/ 2000	24/ 1850	22/ 1700	18/ 1500	16/ 1300	14/ 1150	12/ 1000
	Dist/TAS				212/409	169/404	147/402	132/400	111/397	95/396	82/394	72/393
36000	Time/Fuel			30/ 2250	26/ 2000	23/ 1850	21/ 1700	20/ 1600	17/ 1400	15/ 1250	13/ 1100	12/ 1000
	Dist/TAS			189/405	161/402	143/400	130/398	119/397	102/395	89/393	77/392	68/391
35000	Time/Fuel	35/ 2600	29/ 2250	26/ 2050	23/ 1900	21/ 1750	20/ 1650	19/ 1550	16/ 1350	14/ 1200	13/ 1100	11/ 950
	Dist/TAS	224/407	180/402	157/399	141/397	129/396	119/395	110/394	95/392	83/391	73/390	64/389
34000	Time/Fuel	28/ 2250	25/ 2050	23/ 1900	21/ 1800	20/ 1650	19/ 1550	18/ 1500	16/ 1300	14/ 1200	12/ 1050	11/ 950
	Dist/TAS	173/400	154/397	140/395	128/394	118/393	110/392	102/391	89/389	78/388	69/387	61/386
33000	Time/Fuel	25/ 2100	23/ 1950	21/ 1800	20/ 1700	19/ 1600	18/ 1500	17/ 1450	15/ 1300	13/ 1150	12/ 1050	10/ 900
	Dist/TAS	151/394	138/393	127/391	118/390	109/389	102/388	95/388	84/386	74/385	65/385	58/384
32000	Time/Fuel	23/ 1950	21/ 1850	20/ 1750	19/ 1650	18/ 1550	17/ 1450	16/ 1400	14/ 1250	13/ 1100	11/ 1000	10/ 900
	Dist/TAS	136/390	126/389	117/388	109/387	102/386	95/385	89/384	79/383	70/383	62/382	55/381
31000	Time/Fuel	22/ 1850	20/ 1750	19/ 1650	18/ 1550	17/ 1500	16/ 1400	15/ 1350	13/ 1200	12/ 1100	11/ 1000	10/ 900
	Dist/TAS	125/386	116/385	108/384	101/383	95/382	89/382	84/381	74/380	66/380	59/379	52/378
30000	Time/Fuel	20/ 1800	19/ 1700	18/ 1600	17/ 1500	16/ 1450	15/ 1350	14/ 1300	13/ 1150	12/ 1050	10/ 950	9/ 850
	Dist/TAS	115/382	108/381	101/380	95/379	89/379	84/378	79/378	70/377	62/376	56/376	49/375
29000	Time/Fuel	19/ 1700	18/ 1600	17/ 1550	16/ 1450	15/ 1400	14/ 1300	14/ 1250	12/ 1150	11/ 1000	10/ 900	9/ 850
	Dist/TAS	105/376	98/376	92/375	87/374	82/374	77/374	73/373	65/373	58/372	52/372	46/371
28000	Time/Fuel	17/ 1600	17/ 1550	16/ 1450	15/ 1400	14/ 1300	13/ 1250	13/ 1200	12/ 1100	10/1000	9/ 900	8/ 800
	Dist/TAS	95/371	90/371	84/370	80/370	75/369	71/369	67/369	60/368	54/368	48/367	42/367
27000	Time/Fuel	16/ 1550	15/ 1450	15/ 1400	14/ 1350	13/ 1250	13/ 1200	12/ 1150	11/ 1050	10/ 950	9/ 850	8/ 750
	Dist/TAS	87/366	82/366	77/366	73/365	69/365	66/365	62/364	56/364	50/363	44/363	39/363
26000	Time/Fuel	15/ 1450	15/ 1400	14/ 1350	13/ 1250	13/ 1200	12/ 1150	11/ 1100	10/ 1000	9/ 900	8/ 800	8/ 750
	Dist/TAS	80/362	75/362	71/361	67/361	64/361	60/360	57/360	51/360	46/359	41/359	37/359
25000	Time/Fuel	14/ 1400	14/ 1350	13/ 1250	12/ 1200	12/ 1150	11/ 1100	11/ 1050	10/ 950	9/ 850	8/ 800	7/ 700
	Dist/TAS	73/358	69/357	65/357	62/357	59/357	56/356	53/356	47/356	43/356	38/355	34/355
24000	Time/Fuel	13/ 1350	13/ 1250	12/ 1200	12/ 1150	11/ 1100	11/ 1050	10/ 1000	9/ 900	8/ 850	8/ 750	7/ 700
	Dist/TAS	67/354	63/353	60/353	57/353	54/353	51/353	49/352	44/352	39/352	35/352	32/351
23000	Time/Fuel	13/ 1250	12/ 1200	11/ 1150	11/ 1100	10/ 1050	10/ 1000	10/ 950	9/ 900	8/ 800	7/ 750	7/ 650
	Dist/TAS	61/350	58/350	55/349	53/349	50/349	47/349	45/349	41/348	37/348	33/348	29/348
22000	Time/Fuel	12/ 1200	11/ 1150	11/ 1100	10/ 1050	10/ 1000	9/ 950	9/ 950	8/ 850	8/ 750	7/ 700	6/ 650
	Dist/TAS	56/346	54/346	51/346	48/346	46/345	44/345	42/345	37/345	34/345	30/345	27/344
21000	Time/Fuel	11/ 1150	11/ 1100	10/ 1050	10/ 1000	9/ 950	9/ 950	9/ 900	8/ 800	7/ 750	6/ 700	6/ 600
	Dist/TAS	52/343	49/342	47/342	44/342	42/342	40/342	38/342	35/342	31/341	28/341	25/341
20000	Time/Fuel	10/ 1100	10/ 1050	10/ 1000	9/ 950	9/ 950	8/ 900	8/ 850	7/ 800	7/ 700	6/ 650	6/ 600
	Dist/TAS	47/339	45/339	43/339	41/339	39/339	37/338	35/338	32/338	29/338	26/338	23/338
19000	Time/Fuel	10/ 1050	9/ 1000	9/ 950	9/ 950	8/ 900	8/ 850	8/ 800	7/ 750	6/ 700	6/ 600	5/ 550
	Dist/TAS	43/336	41/336	39/335	37/335	36/335	34/335	32/335	29/335	26/335	24/335	21/335
18000	Time/Fuel	9/ 1000	9/ 950	8/ 900	8/ 900	8/ 850	7/ 800	7/ 800	7/ 700	6/ 650	6/ 600	5/ 550
	Dist/TAS	39/332	38/332	36/332	34/332	33/332	31/332	30/332	27/332	24/332	22/332	19/332
17000	Time/Fuel	9/ 950	8/ 900	8/ 900	8/ 850	7/ 800	7/ 750	7/ 750	6/ 700	6/ 600	5/ 550	5/ 500
	Dist/TAS	36/329	34/329	33/329	31/329	30/329	28/329	27/329	24/329	22/329	20/329	18/329
16000	Time/Fuel	8/ 850	8/ 850	7/ 800	7/ 800	7/ 750	7/ 750	6/ 700	6/· 650	5/ 600	5/ 550	4/ 500
	Dist/TAS	33/326	31/326	30/326	28/326	27/326	26/326	25/326	22/326	20/326	18/326	16/326
15000	Time/Fuel	8/ 850	7/ 800	7/ 800	7/ 750	6/ 750	6/ 700	6/ 650	6/ 600	5/ 550	5/ 550	4/ 450
	Dist/TAS	29/323	28/323	27/323	26/323	24/323	23/323	22/323	20/323	18/323	16/323	15/323
14000	Time/Fuel	7/ 800	7/ 800	7/ 750	6/ 700	6/ 700	6/ 650	6/ 650	5/ 600	5/ 550	4/ 500	4/ 450
	Dist/TAS	26/321	25/321	24/321	23/320	22/320	21/320	20/320	18/320	17/320	15/320	13/320
13000	Time/Fuel	7/ 750	6/ 750	6/ 700	6/ 700	6/ 650	5/ 650	5/ 600	5/ 550	4/ 500	4/ 450	4/ 450
	Dist/TAS	24/318	23/318	22/318	21/318	20/318	19/318	18/318	16/318	15/318	13/318	12/318
12000	Time/Fuel	6/ 700	6/ 700	6/ 650	5/ 650	5/ 600	5/ 600	5/ 550	5/ 500	4/ 500	4/ 450	4/ 400
	Dist/TAS	21/315	20/315	19/315	18/315	18/315	17/315	16/315	15/315	13/315	12/315	11/315
11000	Time/Fuel	6/ 650	5/ 650	5/ 600	5/ 600	5/ 600	5/ 550	5/ 550	4/ 500	4/ 450	4/ 400	3/ 400
	Dist/TAS	19/313	18/313	17/313	16/313	16/313	15/312	14/312	13/312	12/312	11/312	9/312
10000	Time/Fuel	5/ 600	5/ 600	5/ 600	5/ 550	5/ 550	4/ 500	4/ 500	4/ 450	4/ 450	3/ 400	3/ 350
	Dist/TAS	16/310	16/310	15/310	14/310	14/310	13/310	12/310	11/310	10/310	9/310	8/310
8000	Time/Fuel	4/ 500	4/ 500	4/ 500	4/ 500	4/ 450	4/ 450	4/ 450	3/ 400	3/ 350	3/ 350	3/ 300
	Dist/TAS	12/305	11/305	11/305	10/305	10/305	10/305	9/305	8/305	8/305	7/305	6/305
6000	Time/Fuel	4/ 400	4/ 400	3/ 400	3/ 400	3/ 400	3/ 400	3/ 350	3/ 350	3/ 300	2/ 300	2/ 250
	Dist/TAS	8/301	8/301	7/301	7/301	7/301	6/301	6/301	6/301	5/301	5/301	4/301
1500	Time/Fuel	2/ 250	2/ 250	2/ 250	2/ 250	2/ 250	2/ 250	2/ 250	2/ 200	2/ 200	2/ 200	1/ 150

Cruise data may be given graphically or in a table as above. Fuel consumption is often shown in terms of fuel flow against aeroplane mass.

Each aeroplane mass and altitude is related to a NAM value
NAMs are directly related to TAS and time
Fuel consumed is dependent upon aeroplane mass, altitude, TAS, time

CRANFIELD AVIATION TRAINING SCHOOL LTD. PART-FCL ATO N° 276
CATS INNOVATION CENTRE, LUTON, Bedfordshire LU2 8DL U.K.

www.catsaviation.com

7-5

Flight Planning & Monitoring

GROSS WT. KG	0	100	200	300	400	500	600	700	800	900
				CRUISE DISTANCE NAUTICAL AIR MILES						
35000	0	15	30	46	61	77	92	108	123	139
36000	154	170	185	201	216	232	247	263	278	293
37000	309	324	340	355	371	386	401	417	432	448
38000	463	479	494	509	525	540	555	571	586	602
39000	617	632	648	663	678	694	709	725	740	755
40000	771	786	801	817	832	847	862	878	893	908
41000	924	939	954	970	985	1000	1015	1031	1046	1061
42000	1077	1092	1107	1122	1137	1153	1168	1183	1198	1214
43000	1229	1244	1259	1274	1290	1305	1320	1335	1350	1366
44000	1381	1396	1411	1426	1441	1457	1472	1487	1502	1517
45000	1532	1547	1562	1578	1593	1608	1623	1638	1653	1668
46000	1683	1698	1713	1728	1743	1758	1773	1789	1804	1819
47000	1834	1849	1864	1879	1894	1909	1924	1939	1954	1969
48000	1984	1998	2013	2028	2043	2058	2073	2088	2103	2118
49000	2133	2148	2163	2177	2192	2207	2222	2237	2252	2267
50000	2282	2296	2311	2326	2341	2356	2370	2385	2400	2415
51000	2430	2444	2459	2474	2489	2503	2518	2533	2548	2562
52000	2577	2592	2606	2621	2636	2650	2665	2680	2695	2709
53000	2724	2738	2753	2768	2782	2797	2812	2826	2841	2855
54000	2870	2885	2899	2914	2928	2943	2957	2972	2986	3001
55000	3015	3030	3044	3059	3073	3088	3102	3117	3131	3146
56000	3160	3174	3189	3203	3218	3232	3246	3261	3275	3290
57000	3304	3318	3333	3347	3361	3376	3390	3404	3418	3433
58000	3447	3461	3476	3490	3504	3518	3533	3547	3561	3575
59000	3589	3604	3618	3632	3646	3660	3674	3689	3703	3717

Example using CAP 697 Figure 4.5.3.2

Assume mass at start of leg 62 760 kg, leg time 40 minutes, TAS 430 kt, given at the top of Figure 4.5.3.2 and ISA (1)

Enter table at start mass 62 760 kg to obtain →
Start NAM 5 393 (2)

From route plan recall leg time 40 minutes and using TAS from table derive →
NAM for leg 287 (3)

Subtract (3) from (2) to obtain →
End NAM 5 106

Enter table at end NAM to obtain →
End mass 61 000 kg (4)

Subtract end mass (4) from start mass (1) to obtain →
Leg burn off 1 760 kg

If conditions are not ISA (as in this example) apply corrections given below the table

Enter fuel figure in fuel plan

7.9 Descent

The most economic way of operating a jet transport aeroplane is to maintain it at cruise level for as long as possible, leaving a distance for the descent profile that exactly matches the distance required to descend from cruise level to final approach. A descent commenced too early will leave a prolonged flight at low level and this will incur a fuel penalty. A descent that is commenced too late will leave too short a distance and will result in a requirement to indulge in a rapid descent.

CRANFIELD AVIATION TRAINING SCHOOL LTD. PART-FCL ATO N° 276
CATS INNOVATION CENTRE, LUTON, Bedfordshire LU2 8DL U.K.

www.catsaviation.com

7-6

Flight Planning & Monitoring

37000	23	295	98	109	114	114	110
35000	22	290	94	105	110	110	106
33000	21	285	89	99	103	104	101
31000	20	280	83	93	97	98	95
29000	19	275	78	87	91	91	89
27000	19	270	73	81	85	85	83
25000	18	260	68	75	79	79	77
23000	16	255	63	69	72	73	71
21000	15	245	58	64	66	67	66
19000	14	235	53	58	60	61	60
17000	13	225	48	52	54	55	54
15000	12	215	43	46	48	49	48
10000	9	185	30	32	33	34	33
5000	6	140	18	18	18	18	18
3700	5	130	14	14	14	14	14

37000	21	280		100		110	
35000	20	275		96		105	
33000	20	275		91		101	
31000	19	270	76	86		96	
29000	18	265	72	82	88	91	92
27000	17	260	69	78	84	87	87
25000	17	255	64	73	78	80	81
23000	16	250	60	67	72	74	74
21000	15	240	55	62	66	68	68
19000	14	230	51	57	60	62	62
17000	13	225	46	52	55	56	56
15000	12	215	42	46	49	50	50
10000	9	185	30	32	33	34	33
5000	6	140	18	18	18	18	18
3700	5	130	14	14	14	14	14

Enter CAP 697 Figure 4.5.4 at cruise pressure altitude. Go horizontally across to derive time and fuel for descent. These figures are unaffected by aeroplane mass. Air distance for the descent is affected by mass, generally increasing as mass increases. Continue across the horizontal line until intersecting the columns closest to the estimated landing mass to interpolate the NAM value.

Example

An aeroplane, mass at FL330 38000 kg, is to descend at 0.70 M from a cruising altitude of 33 000 ft. Establish the time, fuel and NAM for descent and approach:

Time 20 minutes
Fuel 275 kg
Estimated landing mass 38 000 – 275 kg = 37725 kg
Interpolated value NAM = 83

7.10 Holding

Because of weather or traffic, the arrival of an aircraft at a specific point or airfield may need to be delayed. A procedure is adopted that 'holds' the aeroplane within a defined volume of airspace.

In order to evaluate the requirement to hold consult the route manual to determine the minimum holding fuel required for the sector. Consider other factors such as weather anticipated and likely traffic delays to determine whether additional holding fuel is required. Manufacturers provide tables or graphs giving hold fuel flows for a range of aeroplane masses. A hold is frequently flown at the speed for minimum drag V_{IMD}.

FLAPS UP

Press. Alt. Ft.	WEIGHT 1000 Kg														
	66	64	62	60	58	56	54	52	50	48	46	44	42	40	38
	TOTAL FUEL FLOW KG/HR														
37000					2740	2540	2400	2260	2160	2080	1980	1900	1800	1740	1680
35000		3020	2820	2660	2520	2420	2320	2220	2140	2060	1960	1880	1800	1720	1660
30000	2840	2740	2660	2560	2480	2400	2300	2220	2140	2060	1960	1880	1800	1740	1680
25000	2840	2760	2660	2580	2500	2420	2320	2240	2160	2080	2000	1920	1840	1780	1720
20000	2840	2760	2680	2580	2500	2420	2340	2260	2180	2100	2020	1940	1860	1800	1760
15000	2880	2800	2700	2620	2540	2460	2380	2300	2220	2140	2060	1980	1920	1860	1800
10000	2920	2820	2740	2660	2580	2500	2420	2340	2260	2180	2100	2020	1980	1920	1880
5000	2960	2860	2780	2700	2620	2540	2460	2380	2300	2220	2140	2080	2020	1960	1920
1500	3000	2900	2820	2740	2660	2580	2520	2440	2360	2280	2220	2140	2080	2020	1980

7.11 Other planning procedures

Aeroplane performance manuals address many abnormal operations, including data for planning fuel when:

- Operating with failed engine(s)
- Operating with landing gear extended
- Low level diversion

Self Assessment Test 07

1   (For this question use the Flight Planning Manual MRJT 1 Figure 4.5.3.1)
    Given: flight time from top of climb to the enroute point in FL280 is 48 min. Cruise procedure is long range cruise (LRC).

    Temp. ISA -5° C

    Take-off mass 56 000 kg

    Climb fuel 1 100 kg

    Find: distance in nautical air miles (NAM) for this leg and fuel consumption:
A)   437 NAM; 2100 kg
B)   345 NAM; 2000 kg
C)   350 NAM; 2000 kg
D)   345 NAM; 2100 kg

2   (For this question use the Flight Planning Manual MRJT 1 Figure 4.5.1)
    Given: estimated take-off mass 57 500 kg;
    initial cruise FL 280;
    average temperature during climb ISA -10°C;
    average head wind component 18 kt
    Find: climb time
A)   14 min
B)   13 min
C)   11 min
D)   15 min

3   (For this question use the Flight Planning Manual MRJT 1 Figure 4.5.1)
    Given : brake release mass 57 500 kg
    temperature ISA -10°C; head wind component 16 kt
    initial FL 280

    Find: still air distance (NAM) and ground distance (NM) for the climb
A)   62 NAM; 59 NM
B)   59 NAM;62 NM
C)   67 NAM; 71 NM
D)   71 NAM;67 NM

4   (For this question use the Flight Planning Manual MRJT 1 Figure 4.5.1)
    Given : mass at brake release 57 500 kg;
    temperature ISA -10°C; average head wind component 16 kt
    initial cruise FL 280
    Find: climb fuel
A)   1040 kg
B)   1138 kg
C)   1238 kg
D)   1387 kg

5   (For this question use the Flight Planning Manual MRJT 1 Figure 4.5.3.1)
    Given :FL 330; long range cruise; OAT -63°C; gross mass 50 500 kg.
    Find: true airspeed (TAS)
A)   420 KT
B)   433 KT
C)   431 KT
D)   418 KT

6   (For this question use the Flight Planning Manual MRJT 1 Figure 4.5.3.1)
     Given: long range cruise: temp. -63° C at FL 330
             initial gross mass enroute 54 100 kg; leg flight time 29 min

     Find: fuel consumption for this leg
A)   1680 kg
B)   1093 kg
C)   1200 kg
D)   1100 kg

7   (For this question use the Flight Planning Manual MRJT 1 Figure 4.5.3.1)
     Given: long range cruise; outside air temperature (OAT) -45 ° C in FL 350; mass at the beginning of the
     leg 40 000 kg; mass at the end of the leg 39 000 kg.
     Find: true airspeed (TAS) at the end of the leg and the distance (NAM)
A)   TAS 423 kt; 936 NAM
B)   TAS 431 kt; 227 NAM
C)   TAS 423 kt; 227 NAM
D)   TAS 431 kt; 1163 NAM

8   (For this question use the Flight Planning Manual MRJT 1 Figures 4.2.1, 4.2.2 and 4.5.3.2)
     Given: estimated take-off mass 57 000 kg; still air distance 150 NAM; outside air temperature (OAT) ISA
     -10K; cruise at 0.74 Mach.
     Find : cruise altitude and expected true airspeed
A)   22 000 ft; 441 kt
B)   22 000 ft; 451 kt
C)   25 000 ft; 435 kt
D)   25 000 ft; 445 kt

9   (For this question use the Flight Planning Manual MRJT 1 Figure 4.3.1.B)
     Given : estimated zero fuel mass 50 t; estimated landing mass at alternate 52 t; final reserve fuel 2 t;
     alternate fuel 1 t; flight to destination, distance 720 NM, true course (TC) 030, W/V 340/30; cruise: long
     range FL 330, outside air temperature -30 ° C.
     Find : estimated trip fuel and time
A)   4 800 kg; 01 : 45
B)   4 400 kg; 02 : 05
C)   4 750 kg; 02 : 00
D)   4 600 kg; 02 : 05

Self Assessment Test 07 Answers

1	B
2	B
3	A
4	B
5	A
6	B
7	B
8	C
9	A

CRANFIELD AVIATION TRAINING SCHOOL LTD. PART-FCL ATO N° 276
CATS INNOVATION CENTRE, LUTON, Bedfordshire LU2 8DL U.K.

www.catsaviation.com

7-11

Flight Planning & Monitoring

CHAPTER 8
The Operational fuel flight plan

8.1   Fuel policy

JAR-OPS 1.255 'Fuel Policy', says that
An operator must establish a fuel policy for the purpose of flight planning and in-flight replanning to ensure that every flight carries sufficient fuel for the planned operation and reserves to cover deviations from the planned operation

The planning of flights must only be based on procedures and data contained in or derived from the Operations Manual or current aeroplane specific data and the operating conditions under which the flight is to be conducted including:
- Realistic aeroplane fuel consumption data
- Anticipated masses
- Expected meteorological conditions.
- Air Traffic Services procedures and restrictions

The pre-flight calculation of useable fuel for the flight must include:
- Taxi fuel
- Trip fuel
- Reserve fuel comprising:
- Contingency fuel
- Alternate fuel if a destination alternate is required
- Final reserve fuel
- Additional fuel if required due to the nature of the flight, for example ETOPS

Extra fuel if required by the commander, to take into account special circumstances such as arriving at busy times and waiting in the hold etc.

Taxi fuel should not be less than the amount expected to be used prior to take off. Local conditions at the departure aerodrome and APU consumption should be taken into account.

Trip fuel should include:
- Fuel for take off and climb from aerodrome elevation to initial cruising altitude/level, taking into account the expected departure routing
- Fuel from top of climb to top of descent, including any step climbs along the route
- Fuel from top of descent to the point where the approach is initiated, taking into account the expected arrival procedure
- Fuel for approach and landing at the destination aerodrome

IEM OPS 1.255(c)(3)(i) 'Contingency Fuel', says that

At the planning stage, not all factors which could have an influence on the fuel consumption to the destination aerodrome can be foreseen. Therefore, contingency fuel is carried to compensate for items such as:

>Deviations of an individual aeroplane from the expected fuel consumption data
>Deviations from forecast meteorological conditions
>Deviations from planned routings and/or cruising levels/altitudes

Unless an operator has established an approved a fuel consumption monitoring programme, contingency fuel must be the greater of: 5% of trip fuel or 3% of trip fuel where an en route alternate is available or 5 min at the holding speed at 1500 ft above the destination aerodrome.

Contingency fuel must be the greater of:
5% of trip fuel _or_
3% of trip fuel where an en route alternate is available _or_
5 min at the holding speed at 1500 ft above the destination aerodrome

Alternate fuel must be sufficient for:
- A missed approach from the applicable DH/MDA at destination
- A climb from missed approach to cruising altitude/level
- Cruise from top of climb to top of descent
- Descent from top of descent to the point where an approach is initiated
- Approach and landing

Final reserve fuel is absolutely the final fuel available at final landing, used only if things go badly wrong. It is calculated at holding speed and consumption for 1500 ft above aerodrome elevation in ISA conditions and is based on the estimated mass at arrival over the alternate or the destination if no alternate is required.

IEM OPS 1.255 'Fuel Policy', says that

Final reserve fuel should be fuel to fly for 45 minutes for an aeroplane with reciprocating engines

or

For 30 minutes at holding speed at 1500 ft AAL in ISA for an aeroplane with turbine power units, calculated using estimated mass on arrival at the alternate or destination where no alternate is required

Finally, JAR OPS 1.255(d) requires that in-flight replanning procedures exist for calculating usable fuel required when a flight has to proceed along a route or to another destination other than originally planned.

Line No	STAGE		Temp (C)	Press Alt (ft) X 100	Temp Dev C	WIND		Co (T)	Hd (T)	TAS (kt)	WC (kt)	G/S (kt)	Dist. NGM	Dist. NAM	Time min.	Start Wt	End. Wt.	Fuel Req'd				
	From	To				Dir	Spd																
1.0	A	TOC	----	↗	+05	290	40	130								62000							
2.0	TOTAL DISTANCE – – – – – – – – – – – – – – – →												270										
3.0	TOC	B	-45	330	+06	280	45	130															
4.0	B	C	-48	330	+03	270	50	115						350									
5.0	C	D	-50	330	+01	250	60	090						425									
6.0	D	E	-50	330	+01	240	45	070						350									
7.0	E	TOD	-52	330	-01	240	30	080															
8.0	TOTAL DISTANCE – – – – – – – – – – – – – – →												290										
9.0	TOC	F	----	↘	----	210	30	080															
10	TOTALS																						
11	CONTINGENCY FUEL: ADD																						
12	F	G				240	35	060			+35	190											
13	FINAL TRIP FUEL (inc DIVERSION)																						
14	Holding																						
15	BLOCK FUEL																						

Figure 8.1 The fuel plan

The left side of the fuel plan in Figure 8.1 requires the resolution of a number of wind triangles in order to obtain the individual ground speeds and leg times. Values of TAS are extracted from the flight planning data for the aeroplane. Leg courses and distances are extracted from the operator's library of routes or by measurement or calculation. CAP 697 Figure 4.5.2 enables conversion of nautical ground miles to nautical air miles.

Line No	STAGE		Temp (C)	Press Alt (ft) X 100	Temp Dev C	WIND		Co (T)	Hd (T)	TAS (kt)	WC (kt)	G/S (kt)	Dist. NGM	Dist. NAM	Time min.	Start Wt	End. Wt.	Fuel Req'd			
	From	To				Dir	Spd														
1.0	A	TOC	----	↗	+05	290	40	130	132	382	+38	420	133	110	19	62000	60400	1	6	0	0
2.0	TOTAL DISTANCE – – – – – – – – – – – – – – – – →												270								
3.0	TOC	B	-45	330	+06	280	45	130	133	436	+36	472	157								
4.0	B	C	-48	330	+03	270	50	115	118	433	+44	477	350								
5.0	C	D	-50	330	+01	250	60	090	093	431	+54	485	425								
6.0	D	E	-50	330	+01	240	45	070	071	431	+43	474	350								
7.0	E	TOD	-52	330	-01	240	30	080	080	429	+30	459									
8.0	TOTAL DISTANCE – – – – – – – – – – – – – – – – →												290								
9.0	TOC	F	----	↘	----	210	30	080	083	----					21				2	8	5
10	TOTALS																				
11	CONTINGENCY FUEL: ADD																				
12	F	G				240	35	060	060		+35		190								
13	FINAL TRIP FUEL (inc DIVERSION)																				
14	Holding																				
15	BLOCK FUEL																				

Figure 8.2

8.2 The fuel plan

Example

A turbine-powered aeroplane is to carry sufficient fuel for the following:

- Taxi fuel 400 kg
- Take off and climb to FL330
- Cruise from TOC to TOD at M0.74
- Descent
- Holding fuel sufficient for 45 minutes at 5000 ft
- Flight to alternate
- Contingency fuel 5% of trip fuel (fuel 'A' to 'F')
- Final reserve sufficient for 30 minutes at 1500 ft at the planned alternate

Having considered these requirements one would normally deduct the taxi fuel from the ramp mass in order to obtain the take off mass. This has already been done here so ramp mass is 62 400 kg and take off mass has been entered on the plan. Enter CAP 697 Figure 4.5.1 ISA -5°C to +5°C 'En-route climb' extracting climb time, fuel, distance and TAS.

TAS is used to solve the wind triangle and obtain climb distance (NGM). Enter the climb distance into the plan, subtract it from the first leg distance to obtain distance from TOC to 'B'.

Subtract climb fuel from start mass (62 000 kg) to get mass at TOC.

Determine ISA temperature deviations for each cruise leg.

> Documents for many jet aeroplanes uses Jet Standard Atmosphere in which there is no tropopause and lapse rates continue at 2°C per 1000 ft

CAP 697 provides three cruise tables for 33 000 ft and seventeen tables for M0.74. Refer in this example to CAP 697 Figure 4.5.3.2 M0.74 cruise, 33 000 ft pressure altitude.

TAS is given as 430 kt. This is TAS in ISA but, as the given temperature is not ISA, a correction is applied in accordance with the instructions given at the base of the table. For the leg TOC to 'B' temperature deviation is ISA +6 therefore TAS is increased by 6 knots.

Using this TAS, resolve the wind triangle for the leg, derive groundspeed, time and leg NAM.

Determine the start NAM, end NAM end weight and leg fuel.

Repeat this process for every leg to 'E'.

Using CAP 697 Figure 4.5.4 'Descent' M0.70/280/250 KIAS determine the distance travelled in level cruise from 'E' to TOD.

Trip fuel is the fuel required from take off to 'F'.

Contingency fuel is 5% of trip fuel.

To determine alternate fuel one could use a climb to optimum/short range cruise altitude followed by a cruise (if appropriate) followed by a descent, but this would be a laborious process. The aeroplane's manufacturers provide a means of rapidly determining the diversion fuel.

Refer to CAP 697 Figure 4.3.6. This graph is suitable for use at distances up to 500 nautical miles. Enter at the base with diversion ground distance. Move vertically up to the reference line then to the effective wind component. From here, move vertically to the weight lines selecting the appropriate estimated alternate landing weight. This should be the weight at destination minus the approximate burn off.

In this example enter initially with approximately 53 000 kg obtaining a rough diversion fuel figure of 1 800 kg. Subtract this from the weight at 'F', obtaining a more accurate landing weight at the alternate of 51 100 kg. Re-enter the graph with this weight to determine a fuel burn for the diversion of 1 750 kg. Enter this figure at the fuel plan.

Required holding fuel is 45 minutes at 5000 ft over the planned destination. Refer to CAP 697 Figure 4.4 'Holding Fuel Planning'. Enter with altitude 5 000 ft and weight 53 000 kg, obtaining a fuel flow of 2 420 kg/hour and a holding fuel of 1820 kg.

Final reserve fuel is a minimum of 30 minutes holding fuel at 1500 ft over the alternate. The aeroplane's weight over the alternate can be taken as 50 835 kg. Use this weight in the holding table at 1 500 ft to obtain a fuel flow of approximately 2 390 kg/hour. For 30 minutes this requires a final reserve of 1 195 kg.

Summary

Taxi fuel	400 kg
Take off and climb to FL330	1600 kg
Cruise from TOC to TOD at M0.74	6845 kg
Descent	920 kg
Holding fuel sufficient for 45 minutes at 5000 ft	1810 kg
Flight to alternate	1750 kg
Contingency fuel 5% of trip fuel	470 kg
Final reserve 30 minutes at 1500 ft at alternate	1190 kg
Total Block Fuel	14985 kg

8.3   Fuel tankering

Fuel tankering takes advantage of the differential in fuel costs existing between nations. At an airport where fuel is less expensive, as much fuel as possible is loaded, even if not required for the return flight

The technique balances the differential against the cost of the additional fuel burn as a result of the increased aeroplane mass caused by carrying excess fuel. If the fuel price differential is high and the trip distance short it is normally beneficial to carry the additional fuel. The differential between departure and destination may be shown in the aeroplane route manual as a 'Fuel Cost Index' or simply as a fuel price differential in, say, euro/litre.

8.4   Operating to an isolated or island destination

Where a destination is located on an isolated site or remote island, there may be no suitable alternate airfield if the planned destination becomes unavailable en route. Regulation requires that operators on such routes ensure that:

- The flight does not depart unless the weather at the destination can reasonably be expected to be above limits at the aeroplane's scheduled arrival time
- A fuel monitoring policy exists

IEM OPS 1.250 requires the inclusion in fuel at departure of:
- Taxi fuel
- Trip fuel
- Contingency fuel

Additional fuel not less than isolated airfield (island) reserve
- for reciprocating engine aeroplanes equal to the fuel required at cruising level for 45 minutes plus 15% of trip time or two hours whichever is least and for turbine engine aeroplanes sufficient for flight at cruise consumption for two hours

CHAPTER 9
Charts

9.1   VFR

9.1.1   Overview

We will look at the Jeppesen VFR+GPS chart ED-6 contained in your Student Pilot Route Manual, as this is the chart on which you will be examined. You need to get familiar with this chart, but in practical terms, other VFR charts are basically similar.

Any marking of the chart MUST be erased COMPLETELY. The chart must be unmarked for use in the examination.

Unfold the chart to review it for this section. In the exam, space on your desk is limited, so when you are trying to find a point by latitude and longitude, you may find it useful to find the longitude point first by going through the vertical folds.

From your General Navigation studies, you will know there is much useful information contained along the borders of the chart. Take time to look at these bits of information. When answering questions on this chart, refer to the information contained within these borders- DO NOT ASSUME.

Nations can depart from SARPs if they inform ICAO

Always review the notes and airspace classifications on whatever chart you use. Note the airspace classifications diagrams at the bottom of the ED-6 chart and the markings of such on the topographical depiction.

This area of southern Germany lies along the eastern border of France, the northern Swiss border and the Alps; so note how Minimum Grid Altitudes are marked and the red cross segregating any four such areas every ½ degree in latitude and longitude to assist in determining MSA and cruising levels. With that in mind, the bottom border contains Semi-Circular rules for France and Germany- note the discrepancies.

Meteorological and flight service information is shown, along with frequencies- although in practice one should refer to the AIP. Also, along the right-hand border there is a list of latitude and longitudes, utilising the World Geodetic System 1984 (along the left-hand border you should already have found a note concerning discrepancies). These help in locating reporting points for various control zones, aerodromes and navigation facilities with their respective magnetic variation.

9.1.2   Projection

On the topographical depiction, all the VORs contain an arrow aligned to TRUE north. There are also true north arrows depicted across the chart with the Jeppesen symbol affixed. Top left we see this is a Lambert's Conformal Conic Projection, with standard parallels at 37 and 65 degrees north. Also, the isogonals are as at 1999 values. (There is actually only one on the chart.)

Any straight line drawn on a Lambert's Conformal Conic chart will be a great circle and you will need to read off the true heading with your protractor placed at half distance.

A quick check of the borders where the grid is marked by latitude and longitude gives us an indication of chart convergency, by the inward slope of the meridians.

Convergency = dlong x Sin Mean Latitude
= 6° 50' x Sin 48° 10'
= 6° 50' x 0.745
= 5° 05' across the chart

9.1.3   Aerodromes

Lets take a look at the Aerodrome information. We shall start at AUSBURG, ICAO identifier EDMA. If we look at the right-hand border notes, it is located at N48° 25.5' E010° 55.9'. It is situated within a class D CTR, the horizontal limits of which are pictorially portrayed and extending vertically to 3100 feet AMSL. Within this CTR are two information blocks. The first lists the airfield name and associated navigation aid details. (You should from your Radio Navigation studies be able to determine which frequency belongs to which navigation aid.) The other lists the ICAO identifier, the elevation of the aerodrome in feet (1515 feet amsl) and the length of the longest runway in meters (1280 meters) -DO NOT CONFUSE THESE TWO! Also listed is the tower frequency. The small, bracketed 'v' denotes that a VDF service is available at Ausburg.

Located on the aerodrome are an NDB and a DME, the details of which are tabulated in the right-hand border.

Always obtain authoritive Navigation Aid information from the AIP

The CTR is surrounded by various VFR and TMA transit reporting points (November, Oscar etc.), the full list of which is again listed in the chart borders. There are also some man-made obstructions to be aware of, for example a lit tower at the northwest corner of the CTR, extending to 2411 feet amsl just north of waypoint Whiskey 1. It is situated on rising ground up to 1637 feet and the Grid MSA is 3800 feet in this area. At this point, refer again to the notes on MSA in the left-hand border- particularly to the reasons behind providing 1000 foot clearance or 2000 foot clearance.

Always account for raised obstructions 5 NM either side of track when determining MSA for any route

This grid MSA may not be your REQUIRED MSA. The grid accounts for an area extending 30 minutes of latitude, i.e. 30 NM.

Finally, encircling Ausburg is an area cautioning the need to set the transponder to mode A or C if we have the facility and squawk code 0021.

9.1.4   Other Airspace

Moving away from the aerodrome, we need to note overlapping airspace restrictions associated with Munich to the east, also gliding at Aichach. There is an area of Danger, Restricted or Prohibited airspace to the north- ED(R)-140. This extends from a base of FL60 to an upper limit of FL100.

1 hPa = 27 feet

We can see that this is a permanent area as it does not contain the note NOTAM.

(See area ED(R)-130, south of Stuttgart.)

The note north of Ausburg concerning Munich Radar on a frequency of 131.22Mhz is for entry into Munich's class C airspace from this quadrant. Note the other three corners of this airspace- the frequencies could be different.

The highest point on the chart? To the south at E012° 20'

CRANFIELD AVIATION TRAINING SCHOOL LTD. PART-FCL ATO N° 276
CATS INNOVATION CENTRE, LUTON, Bedfordshire LU2 8DL U.K.   www.catsaviation.com

9-2   Flight Planning & Monitoring

9.2   IFR

Radio Navigation charts, are usually referred to as Enroute Charts. These come in various forms and as before, we will concentrate on the Jeppesen charts from your JAR Student Pilot Route Manual.

Have a look through the selection in the manual. They are divided into two sections:

ENROUTE - Consisting of Europe Low E(LO)1 to 5, Atlantic Orientation AT(H/L)1 and 2, US(LO)45 to 48.

HIGH - Consisting of Europe High E(HI)1 to 4, CAA Examination Chart E(HI)4 and 5 (Do not confuse with the standard E(HI)4 and 5 opposite during the exam! Read the question), Canada/Alaska CA(HI)3 and 4, US(HI)3 and 4, Atlantic Polar High AT(HI)5, North Canada Plotting Chart, North America Plotting Chart 27th edition, North Atlantic Plotting Chart 24 Dec 1999.

Similarities mean that once you have a basic understanding, you will be able to find your way around any Jeppesen chart.

Take time to have a look through the introduction section, to familiarise yourself with the chart glossary and legend. Do not concern yourself with SIDs and STARs at this time as they are covered in a later section.

We will start with Europe low altitude chart E(LO)2.

By simply undoing the first fold, you will see a fair amount of information to begin with. Principly note the placement map and summertime to UTC reference. Turn the chart over and note that you can quickly find major airports by going through the top folds. (Although this is only of any practical use operationally).

Open the chart and as a double check, when open see that it is actually chart E(LO)2 you are open at, firstly by checking the top corners and secondly- is it the area you were expecting? It is easy in the exam to lose valuable minutes on the wrong side of a chart!

You will note that there is only basic coastline information from a topographical viewpoint, re-enforcing its use as a radio navigation chart, but plotting is a viable option as we shall see later. At the top you will see a nautical mile scale. Measure distances against this as opposed to using the 1"/5 NM conversion.

Accuracy is of paramount importance when plotting

The meridians are only scaled to 10 minutes of latitude. Top right we see it uses a Lamberts projection, along with other details we need to know for plotting purposes. (You will be required to do some plotting on some of these charts during the exam).

Across the top and bottom borders are 'flecks' to mark magnetic variation. Also dotted across most of the chart are numbered notes in boxes. These refer to particular areas and/or tracks. There really is no east way to do this, but when following a track, you may come across a number referring to one of these notes. They are not placed in any discernable order, you simply have to hunt for it; but they have import, as we will find out later.

To view what information is available to us on this chart, we will begin planning a flight from Cork in southern Ireland to Brussels. We shall use airway G1 from Strumble on the western Welsh coast to do so. Starting at top left of the chart, you will find Cork aerodrome. We can see localiser front course information, marker frequencies and idents, plus the aerodrome elevation of 502 feet amsl.   The VOR is situated on the aerodrome and forms a compulsory reporting point for both airways G4 and B4. From the VOR information box we see CRK has a co-located DME, is situated at N51° 50.4' W008° 29.7' and it's ident in morse code is represented. Magnetic variation is 7°W. The aerodrome CTR takes in an NDB at the Old Head of Kinsale lighthouse and to the north and south are danger areas with upper and lower limits plus additional information (EI(D)-13 is active weekdays by NOTAM). Other danger/restricted areas are expanded on in the left-hand border of the chart.

Each box formed by 1 degree of latitude and longitude contains a grid Minimum Off-Route Altitude (MORA). Cork is within an area with a MORA of 3300 feet. A +/- after the number would indicate doubtful accuracy, such as in polar regions. The shaded line marked '1' to the south indicates this area overlaps with chart E(LO)1.

So, lets depart Cork and pick up airway B10 on CRK radial 094. Around the box indicating this is airway B10, we see a Minimum En-Route Altitude (MEA) of 6000 feet and a MORA of 2000 feet (indicated by an 'a'). The track distance to Non-Compulsory/Request Only Waypoint BANBA, situated at N51° 57.2' W006° 14.4' is 84 nautical miles. The total distance to the next facility, Strumble VOR/DME, is 128 NM; this we can see is a further 44 NM no from BANBA. Passing BANBA, our MEA goes up to FL130, so the best flight level to fly this entire airway would be FL130 eastbound on QNE.

> **Always check MEA along your entire route before deciding on an Altitude or Flight level**

As we pass BANBA, we enter London FIR class G airspace. Our inbound course to STU VOR is now 093° (radial 273). Look at the top border of the chart and note that the magnetic variation in the area is now 6°W.

> **VORs are aligned to Magnetic North. Always check the Magnetic Variation**

We turn onto 109° and pick up airway G1 with 68 NM to go to BRECON VOR with waypoint AMMAN 40 NM along Track. Next STU45 and STU53 you will note are respectively 45 NM and 53 NM from STRUMBLE VOR. These are mileage breaks and not waypoints for use in ATS flight planning or communications. You would though see them displayed on a 737 Navigation Display and be able to enter them into the Flight Management Computer. Above our airway line you will see airway G1 and have noted the 500' discrepancy. If you do not understand why, please review your semi-circular rules before proceeding. At BRECON, airway A25 crosses north to south and vice versa, but note that northbound it is available at even levels only, denoted by the 'E' and arrow.

Overhead BRECON, we take up a heading of 105° magnetic toward non-compulsory waypoint ALVIN. This is situated 22 DME from BRECON (note the D and →). To the south is FILTON NDB 'OF'. This facility is not continuous (denoted by the *), so check NOTAMS for timings. Next comes waypoint WOTAN and then MALBY, which is 32 DME from COMPTON VOR/DME.

After passing COMPTON, we track 105°M for 4 NM to reach waypoint NORRY. We can confirm reaching as we should be on the BOVINGDON 240° radial at 26 DME. Next comes BIGGIN HILL VOR/DME- note that under the information box for WOODLEY NDB that airway G1 disregards WOD as a waypoint.

Before leaving BIG VOR and heading on to DVR, we need to review notes '2' and '40'.
Remember we started at FL130 and therefore note '40' applies to us. But we did not depart from the UK, so can continue on G1. From Dover, we enter the Channel, where G1 becomes a one-way airway- or does it? Review the extra notes marked here.

Overhead KOSKY, we have a compulsory reporting point, but review note '14' before being sure you are overhead. Onward to MACKEL on 106° M and then to the compulsory reporting point at DENDER NDB. Note that within the information box, 'DEN' is underlined. This means we need to use the Beat Frequency Oscillator swith on the ADF to receive the ident.

By now we should have begun our decent into Brussels National airport. Have a look across the chart at other routes and get an idea of the other forms of symbology.

Self Assessment Test 09

1 (Refer to the Route Manual VFR+GPS chart ED-6). An aeroplane is flying VFR and approaching position TANGO VORTAC (48°37'N, 009°16'E) at FL 055 and magnetic course 090°, distance from VORTAC TANGO 20 NM. Name the frequency of the TANGO VORTAC.
A) 422 kHz
B) 118.80 MHz
C) 112.50 MHz
D) 118.60 MHz

2 (Refer to the Route Manual VFR+GPS chart ED-6). Give the name and frequency of the Flight Information Service for an aeroplane in position (47°59'N, 010°14'E).
A) MEMMINGEN INFORMATION 122.1 MHz
B) MÜNCHEN INFORMATION 126.95 MHz
C) MÜNCHEN INFORMATION 120.65 MHz
D) FRANKFURT INFORMATION 128.95 MHz

3 (Refer to the Route Manual VFR+GPS chart ED-6). Flying from SAULGAU airport (48°02'N, 009°31'E) to ALTENSTADT airport (47°50'N, 010°53'E). Find magnetic course and the distance.
A) Magnetic course 282°, distance 56 NM
B) Magnetic course 102°, distance 82 NM
C) Magnetic course 078°, distance 82 NM
D) Magnetic course 102°, distance 56 NM

4 (Refer to the Route Manual VFR+GPS chart ED-6). Give the frequency of STUTTGART ATIS.
A) 112.250 MHZ
B) 126.125 kHz
C) 126.125 MHz
D) 135.775 MHz

5 (Refer to the Route Manual VFR+GPS chart ED-6). Which navigation aid is located in position 48°30'N, 007°34'E?
A) NDB
B) VOR
C) TACAN
D) VOR/DME

6 (Refer to Route Manual VFR+GPS chart ED-6). Flying VFR from VILLINGEN (48°03.5'N, 008°27.0'E) to FREUDENSTADT (48°28.0'N, 008°24.0'E) determine the distance.
A) 24 NM
B) 46 NM
C) 28 NM
D) 24 km

7 (Refer to Route Manual VFR+GPS chart ED-6). Flying VFR from VILLINGEN (48°03.5'N, 008°27.0'E) to FREUDENSTADT (48°28.0'N, 008°24.0'E).Determine the minimum altitude within a corridor 5 NM left and 5 NM right of the courseline in order to stay 1000 ft clear of obstacles.
A) 4200 ft
B) 1500 ft
C) 3900 ft
D) 2900 ft

CRANFIELD AVIATION TRAINING SCHOOL LTD. PART-FCL ATO N° 276

CATS CATS INNOVATION CENTRE, LUTON, Bedfordshire LU2 8DL U.K.

www.catsaviation.com

9-5

Flight Planning & Monitoring

Self Assessment Test 09 Answers

1	C
2	B
3	D
4	C
5	D
6	A
7	C

CRANFIELD AVIATION TRAINING SCHOOL LTD. PART-FCL ATO N° 276
CATS INNOVATION CENTRE, LUTON, Bedfordshire LU2 8DL U.K.

www.catsaviation.com

9-6

Flight Planning & Monitoring

CHAPTER 10

Standard Instrument Departures (SIDS) and Standard Terminal Arrival Routes (STARS)

10.1 Air traffic services (ATS) routes

An ATS Route is a specified route designated by the appropriate ATS authority for channelling the flow of traffic as necessary for the provision of air traffic services (ICAO annex 2)

The term ATS route means variously:

- Airway
- Advisory route
- Controlled or uncontrolled route
- Arrival or departure route

SIDs and STARs depict a procedure and therefore not to scale.

These are referred to as 'Plates' and are constructed to display the Lateral and Vertical profiles of departure and arrival, to reduce ATC communications. They show requirements in both height/altitude and speed so as to maintain the safe and orderly flow of air traffic.

Example: Heathrow N051°28.6' W000°27.6' to Munich N048°21.3' E011° 47.3'

10.2 Standard instrument departure (SID)

Before joining the ATS routing, the correct departure procedure leaving London Heathrow must be followed. The Jeppesen Student Pilot Route Manual shows several SIDs for London Heathrow. Departure runway and route direction determine the appropriate one and the SID you are required to use will be issued by ATS with your clearance. London Heathrow has parallel runways 09R/27L and 09L/27R as well as a minor runway 05/23.That departure selected here is called DOVER THREE GOLF, ('DVR 3G', plate 10-3E) and is suitable for take off from runway 27L.

CRANFIELD AVIATION TRAINING SCHOOL LTD. PART-FCL ATO N° 276
CATS INNOVATION CENTRE, LUTON, Bedfordshire LU2 8DL U.K.
10-1

www.catsaviation.com
Flight Planning & Monitoring

10.2.1   *Lateral profile*

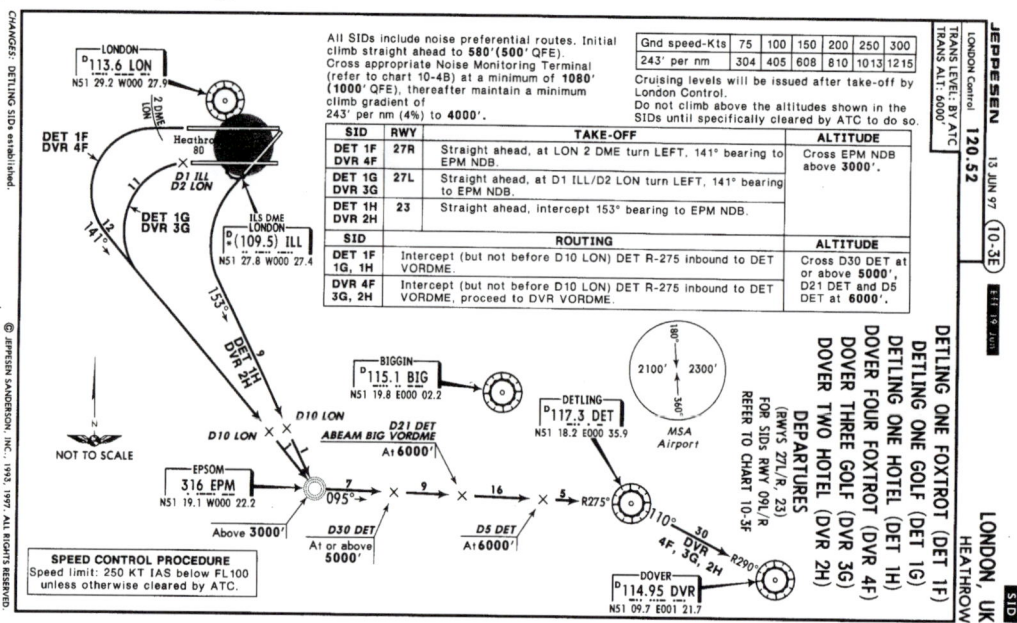

Figure 10.1 London Heathrow DVR 3G departure lateral profile

Observe the path as viewed from above, which is marked by either distance breaks, which are indicated by an 'x', or by a radio navigation aid and/or radial/DME from such. There is a circle to indicate MSA, in this case there are two depending on your location west or east of the airport and the radial that divides the two.

Always check all information on a procedural chart before acting on it

There is much text which MUST be read in full to gain the whole picture of what is required by the aircrafts path. For all the SIDs on this plate, there is a noise procedure with height requirements and a table to the right, which assists the pilot in checking compliance.

A speed control box is at bottom left. The main box at centre re-affirms the diagrammatic representation.

10.2.2   *Procedure*

From runway 27L, climb straight ahead to 1 DME from ILL, which is 2 DME from LON VOR. Turn left to intercept track 141° toward EPM NDB. Having reached at least 10 DME from LON, we can commence a turn to the left to intercept the 275 radial from DET VOR/DME. We must be above 3000' passing EPM. Now we make good a track of 095°, climbing so as to be at or above 5000' at 30 DME from DET, at 6000' abeam BIG VOR/DME and not to climb above 6000' on QNH (as we have not climbed above the transition altitude of 6000'), until we reach DET.

We can see in the notes that we may be given specific permission to climb above these altitudes by ATC; this also applies to the speed restriction.
Above DET, we turn right to track 110° into DVR VOR/DME on the 290 radial.

Distances involved in this routing are shown on the chart:
From take off to EPM NDB	11 + 1 = 12 NM
From EPM NDB to DET VORDME	7 + 9 + 16 + 5 = 37 NM
From DET VORDME to DVR VORDME	30 NM
Total	79 NM

CRANFIELD AVIATION TRAINING SCHOOL LTD. PART-FCL ATO N° 276
CATS INNOVATION CENTRE, LUTON, Bedfordshire LU2 8DL U.K.

www.catsaviation.com

10-2

Flight Planning & Monitoring

10.2.3 Vertical profile

For noise abatement the initial climb is to 580 ft on QNH (500 ft on QFE) to cross the Noise Monitoring Terminal at or above 1080 ft on QNH (1000 ft QFE), thereafter maintaining a climb gradient of at least 243 ft per NM (4%). Subsequently minimum altitudes (on QNH) are:

Overhead EPM NDB	above 3000'
At 30 DME from DET VOR/DME	at or above 5000'
At 21 DME from DET VOR/DME	at 6000'
At 05 DME from DET VOR/DME	at 6000'

You should refer to plate 10-4B at this stage for more information.

10.2.4 Speed restriction

Speed is limited to 250 KIAS below FL100 (pressure altitude 10 000 ft).

10.3 Standard terminal arrival route (STAR)

STARs provide transition from the en route structure to a holding fix or an instrument approach fix/arrival waypoint in the terminal area

For arrival into Munich from the west, we have received clearance for an AALEN 1T procedure. Select plate 10-2B.

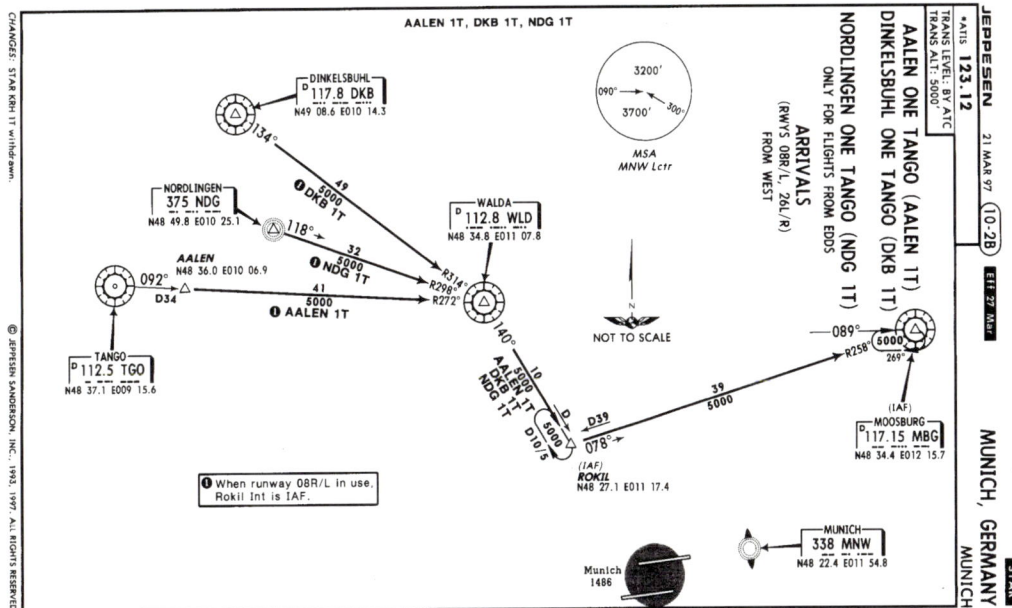

Figure 10.2 Lateral Profile

From non-compulsory airspace fix AALEN (TGO radial 092, 34DME), maintain the 272° radial from WLD, which is the 092° radial from TGO, to overhead WLD. At WLD turn right to intercept the 140° radial to 10 DME (non-compulsory airspace fix ROKIL) to hold, if required, or proceed on course 078°M to MBG. On this occasion, note that the MSA is centred on the MNW NDB/locator.

Minimum en route altitude from AALEN to MBG is 5000' and if we look at the notes on the plate, we see that depending on which runway is in use, the IAF changes, it being MBG for runways 26 L/R and ROKIL for runways 08 L/R. We can see why by the position of the Airfield, although again, these are a procedural depiction and not to scale.

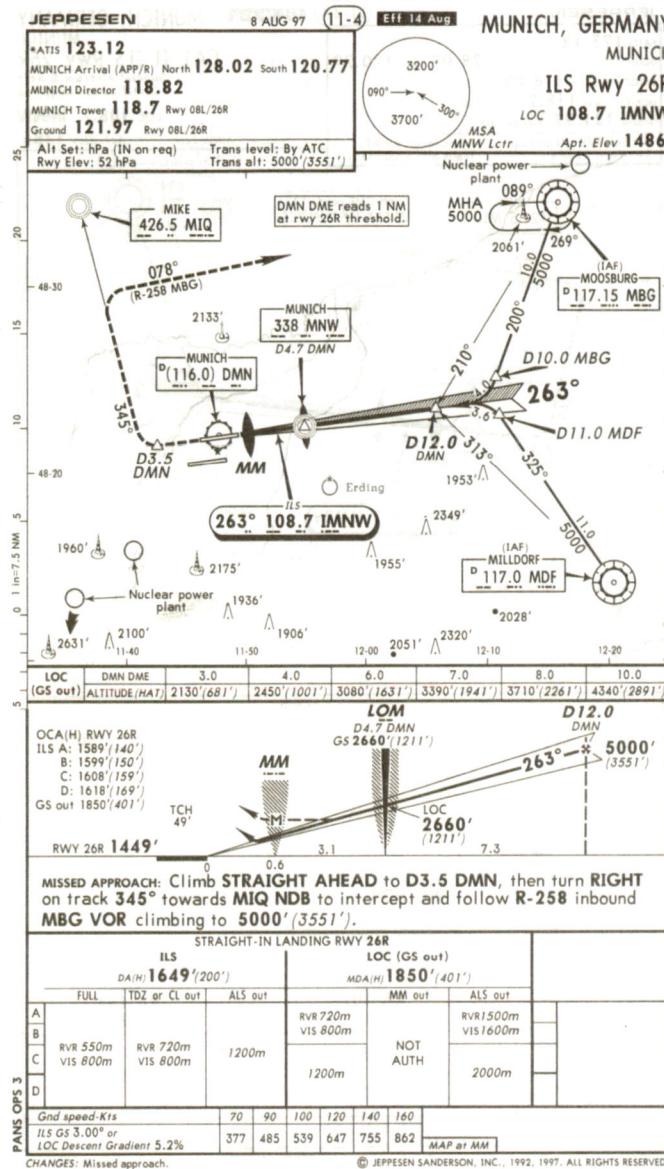

Figure 10.3 Approach

Approach charts are graphic illustrations of instrument approach procedures prescribed by the governing authority

For this example, we are expecting runway 26R to be in use and that an ILS approach is anticipated. Refer to plate 11-4.

A right turn is made at initial approach fix MBG to maintain the 200° radial to DME range 10 NM, still at 5000 ft, where a further right turn is made to establish on the localiser inbound course 263°. The highest obstacle on the chart is marked by a bold arrow; in this case a tower to the southwest which is 2631' tall.

At final approach fix (FAF) range 12 NM from DMN DME, 11 NM from the runway threshold since a note informs us that DMN reads 1 NM at 26R threshold. Descent on glideslope is commenced from 5000 ft QNH. Height above threshold (HAT) since this is a precision approach is 3551'. The maltese cross denotes this to be the FAF.

CRANFIELD AVIATION TRAINING SCHOOL LTD. PART-FCL ATO N° 276
CATS INNOVATION CENTRE, LUTON, Bedfordshire LU2 8DL U.K.

www.catsaviation.com

10-4

Flight Planning & Monitoring

At locator outer marker (LOM) MNW, 3.7 NM from runway threshold (remember the displaced threshold), a check altitude is 2660 ft (HAT 1211 ft). A middle marker (MM) is 0.6 NM from runway threshold and serves as the missed approach point (M) in the event of a localiser only (GS out) non-precision approach. The dotted line leading up to the missed approach point indicates the Minimum Descent Altitude/Height.

In a block at the base of the profile view, check heights are given for a number of ranges from DMN DME.

The missed approach procedure is given with the salient points in bolt italics, to complement the graphic depiction on both lateral and vertical profiles.

Minima are given for a straight-in landing on runway 26R for ICAO aircraft approach categories A to D. Decision altitude (DA) is 1649', equivalent to decision height (DH) 200' and minimum descent altitude (MDA) in the event of a localiser only (GS out) approach is 1850'. Minimum runway visual range (RVR) and meteorological visibility (VIS) are specified variously for full facilities, touchdown zone (TDZ) or centreline (CL) lighting out and approach lighting system (ALS) out, for ILS and LOC(GS out) respectively. Note that non-precision approaches without a middle marker are not authorised.

A speed table at the bottom of the page relates aircraft approach speeds to the rate of descent for the ILS glideslope (descent in feet per minute) and, since for this procedure a non-precision approach descent gradient is coincidental, it relates speed to the distance shown from the final approach fix to the missed approach point.

10.4 Other airport charts

- Noise abatement departure procedures
- Runway crossing procedures and runway holding areas, backed by category 2/3 ILS operation procedures and movements information
- Airport plan
- Latitude and Longitude co-ordinates at stand and apron positions, used for INS or GNSS on suitably equipped aircraft
- Engine starting, taxi, parking and stand entry procedures
- Use of runways for landing

Self Assessment Test 10

1 Refer to the Route Manual chart SID PARIS Charles-De-Gaulle (20-3))
Planning a IFR flight from Paris (Charles de Gaulle) to London (Heathrow).
Find the elevation of the departure aerodrome.
A) 217 ft.
B) 2 ft
C) 387 ft
D) 268 ft

2 (Refer to the Route Manual chart STAR LONDON Heathrow (10-2))
Planning a IFR flight from Paris (Charles de Gaulle) to London (Heathrow).
Find the elevation of the destination aerodrome.
A) 77 ft
B) 177 ft
C) 100 ft
D) 80 ft

3 (Refer to the Route Manual SID chart 20-3 for PARIS Charles-de-Gaulle)
Planning an IFR-flight from Paris to London.

Determine the distance of the departure route ABB 8A.
A) 72.5 NM
B) 56 NM
C) 83 NM
D) 74.5 NM

4 (Refer to the Route Manual SID chart 20-3 for PARIS Charles-de-Gaulle)
Planning an IFR-flight from Paris (Charles de Gaulle) RWY 27 to London.
Given: Distance from PARIS Charles-de-Gaulle to top of climb 50 NM
Determine the distance from the top of climb (TOC) to ABB 116.6.
A) 36.5 NM
B) 31 NM
C) 24.5 NM
D) 33 NM

5 (Refer to the Route Manual chart E(HI)4 CAA-Edition, STAR 10-2 and Instrument approach chart 11-4
ILS DME Rwy 27R for London Heathrow)
Planning an IFR-flight from Paris to London (Heathrow).
Assume: STAR is BIG 2A, Variation 5° W, en-route TAS 430 kts, W/V 280/40, descent distance 76NM.
Determine the magnetic course, ground speed and wind correction angle from ABB 116.6(N50 08.1
E001 51.3) to top of descent.
A) MC 319°, GS 396 kt, WCA -3°
B) MC 141°, GS 396 kt, WCA -3°
C) MC 321°, GS 396 kt, WCA -3°
D) MC 141°, GS 396 kt, WCA +3°

CRANFIELD AVIATION TRAINING SCHOOL LTD. PART-FCL ATO N° 276
CATS INNOVATION CENTRE, LUTON, Bedfordshire LU2 8DL U.K.

www.catsaviation.com

10-6

Flight Planning & Monitoring

Self Assessment Test 10 Answers

1	C
2	D
3	D
4	C
5	C

CRANFIELD AVIATION TRAINING SCHOOL LTD. PART-FCL ATO N° 276
CATS INNOVATION CENTRE, LUTON, Bedfordshire LU2 8DL U.K.

www.catsaviation.com

10-7

Flight Planning & Monitoring

CHAPTER 11

Point of Equal Time (PET) and Point of Safe Return (PSR)

11.1 Point of equal time

There exists a point along track at which the time to continue to destination is equal to the time to return to the point of departure. If an emergency occurred before this point the aeroplane should turn back. If an emergency occurred after this point the aeroplane should continue flying to it's destination. Knowing points of equal time (PET)s in advance allows an instant decision to be made in an emergency situation.

Point of Equal Time may also be referred to as Critical Point (CP).

The PET is that point at which it would take equal time to continue to destination or to return to the point of departure

PETs may be calculated for flight with all engines operating and one or more engine(s) inoperative.

There exists an all engines PET and one or more engine(s) inoperative PET

The following relationship exists between distance, speed and time:

Distance = Speed x Time	Time = $\dfrac{Distance}{Speed}$

Route distance along track is fixed, but speed will vary depending on wind velocity and the contingency for which we are planning.

Example:
Consider the route from KUJACK (N58° 05.8' W068° 25.6') to LA GRANDE RIVIERE (N53° 37.5' W077° 43.0'), as depicted on chart CA (HI) 3

The distance from YVP to YGL along airway J535 is 411 NM. In still air, the PET is halfway along the airway ie. 411 / 2 = 205.5 NM along track. In still air, This distance is independent of speed.

If we now consider the effect of a wind velocity of 270 / 45, we get a different picture:

Using the Multi-engine piston (MEP) from CAP 697, we have a maximum fuel load of 123 USG. Using the endurance table, with reserve at 15000' on economy setting, we have an endurance of 4hrs 25mins (4.41hrs). In ISA, our TAS is 184 KT (fig. 3.4).

At this TAS, our groundspeed to YGL is 130 KT after application of wind on the CRP-5; but our return groundspeed to YVP is 216 KT.

Obviously our leg times are now different, out and back, to our "still air" PET:

Time YVP to "still air" PET = 3 h 9 min
Time "still air" PET to YVP = 1 h 58 min

CRANFIELD AVIATION TRAINING SCHOOL LTD. PART-FCL ATO N° 276
CATS INNOVATION CENTRE, LUTON, Bedfordshire LU2 8DL U.K.

www.catsaviation.com

11-1

Flight Planning & Monitoring

So, our PET is no longer such.

FORMULA

Let:
- D be total route distance
- d be the distance from origin to the PET

Therefore, D – d is the distance from the PET to destination

Let:
- be groundspeed out to PET/destination
- H be groundspeed home to origin from PET

$O = groundspeed\ A\ to\ B$
$H = Groundspeed\ B\ to\ A$

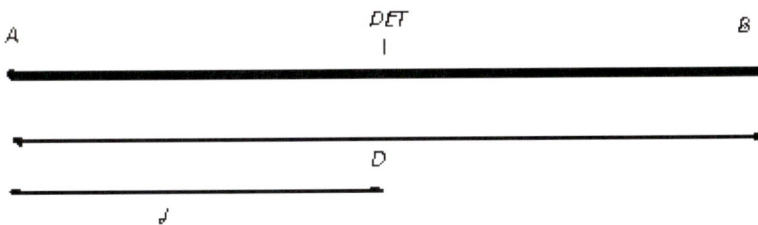

Figure 11.1

Time PET to A must equal time PET to B, where time = $\dfrac{distance}{speed}$

So: $\dfrac{d}{H} = \dfrac{(D-d)}{O}$

Cross-multiplying:

O x d	= H x (D – d)
Od	= HD – Hd
Od + Hd	= HD
d x (O + H)	= HD

Giving:

$$\text{Distance to PET} = \frac{DH}{O+H}$$

CRANFIELD AVIATION TRAINING SCHOOL LTD. PART-FCL ATO N° 276
CATS INNOVATION CENTRE, LUTON, Bedfordshire LU2 8DL U.K.

www.catsaviation.com

11-2

Flight Planning & Monitoring

Example

Now, using this formula, lets apply it to our flight to determine our PET with the wind applied.

Groundspeed out (O)   = 152 KT
Groundspeed home (H) = 221 KT
Distance (D)   = 411 NM

Therefore:

$$\frac{411 \times 221}{152 + 221} = \frac{90831}{373} = 243.51 \text{ NM}$$

The PET is now beyond the mid way point, due to the fact that we are talking in terms of TIME and not distance in the first instance. This we can prove:

From PET to LA GRANDE RIVIERE (YGL)

411 – 243.51 = 164.49 NM, at 152 KT = 66 min

From PET to KUJACK (YVP)

243.51 NM at 221 KT = 66 min

This is all fine if we are dealing with an emergency other than that involving the condition of the aircraft. If we now talk in terms of engine failure or loss of pressurisation, which involves descent to a lower level and in both cases a lower true airspeed, we get another picture again.

Single-engine TAS = 113 KT (90 KT RAS, 15000' at -15 $^{\circ}$C)
Groundspeed home (H) with W/V 270/45 = 153 KT
Groundspeed out (O) remains 152 KT until point of failure.

$$\frac{411 \times 153}{152 + 153} = \frac{62883}{305} = 206.17 \text{NM}$$

Our PET has now moved closer to our point of departure due to the lower return groundspeed.

As this is our worst-case scenario, PET is worked out using the single-engine return option or loss of pressurisation, depending on the type of aircraft.

CRANFIELD AVIATION TRAINING SCHOOL LTD. PART-FCL ATO N° 276
CATS CATS INNOVATION CENTRE, LUTON, Bedfordshire LU2 8DL U.K.

www.catsaviation.com

11-3

Flight Planning & Monitoring

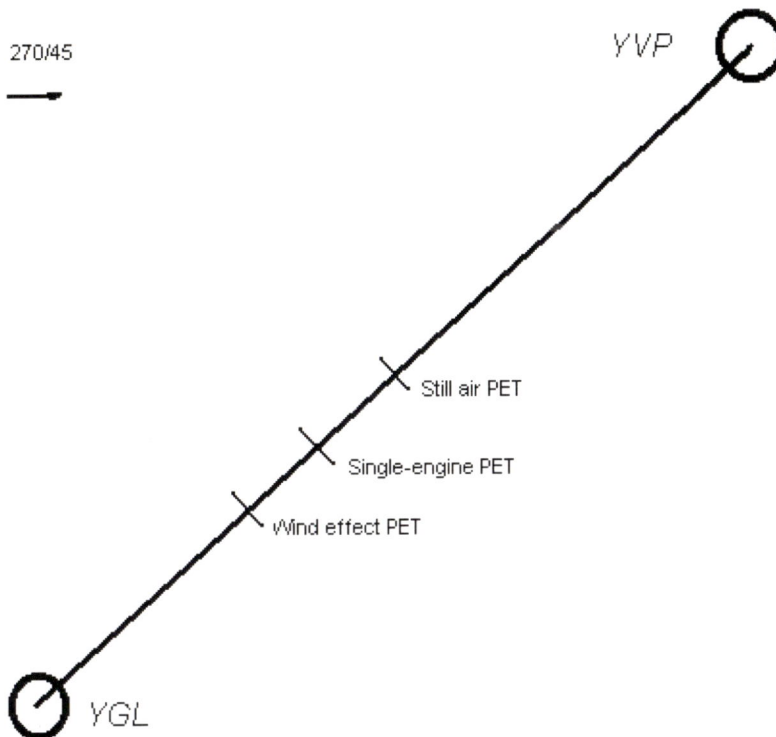

270/45

YVP

Still air PET

Single-engine PET

Wind effect PET

YGL

Figure 11.2

As a gross error check, the wind blows AWAY from the end of track to which the PET is closer. So, if we depart with a tailwind, we can expect the PET to be before the halfway point. Likewise, with a headwind outbound, it should be beyond halfway.

> In other than still air, the PET moves into wind, wind having more effect as TAS reduces.

11.2 Point of Safe Return (PSR)

> The Point of Safe Return (PSR) is the farthest point along track to which an aeroplane can fly and still return to the point of departure with the required fuel reserve

The PSR used to be called the Point of No Return (PNR). There is a strong distinction between the PSR and PET; you may already have passed your PET but still not have reached your PSR.

> The PET concerns TIME
> The PSR concerns ENDURANCE

Lets look at a Boeing 747-400 flying Heathrow to Los Angeles. It may have a PET worked out between Shannon in Ireland and Gander in Newfoundland for it's Atlantic crossing, but it's PSR to return to London may be farther into Canada due to it's fuel load and the number of diversionary aerodromes available over the United States not necessitating a PET after leaving MNPS airspace.

11.2.1   Formulae Method

As with the PET, the object is to find a point along our route, this time using our fuel endurance as the limiting factor. As endurance is a function of time and it stands to reason that it will take the same time to fly out to the PSR as it will to return from it, we can therefore substitute Endurance (E) for Distance (D) in our equation:

Therefore:

$$\text{Time to PSR} = \frac{E \times H}{O + H}$$

Example

We will use our flight from KUJACK to LA GRANDE RIVIERE to look at the PSR in practice.

From the CAP 697, we found our endurance was 4 h 25 min (4.41h)

You will remember out PET was 206.17 NM along track. Our PSR on the other hand:

$$\frac{4.41 \times 153}{152 + 153} = \frac{674.73}{305} = 2.21 \text{ h} \ (2 \text{ h } 12 \text{ min})$$

2.21 h at 152 KT = 335.9 NM

Again, we use the single-engine / pressurisation failure TAS for the 'H' component of the equation to account for the worst-case scenario.

Distance to PSR may also be calculated using the following formula:

$$\text{Distance to PSR} = \frac{EOH}{O + H}$$

11.3 CRP-5 Method

11.3.1 PET

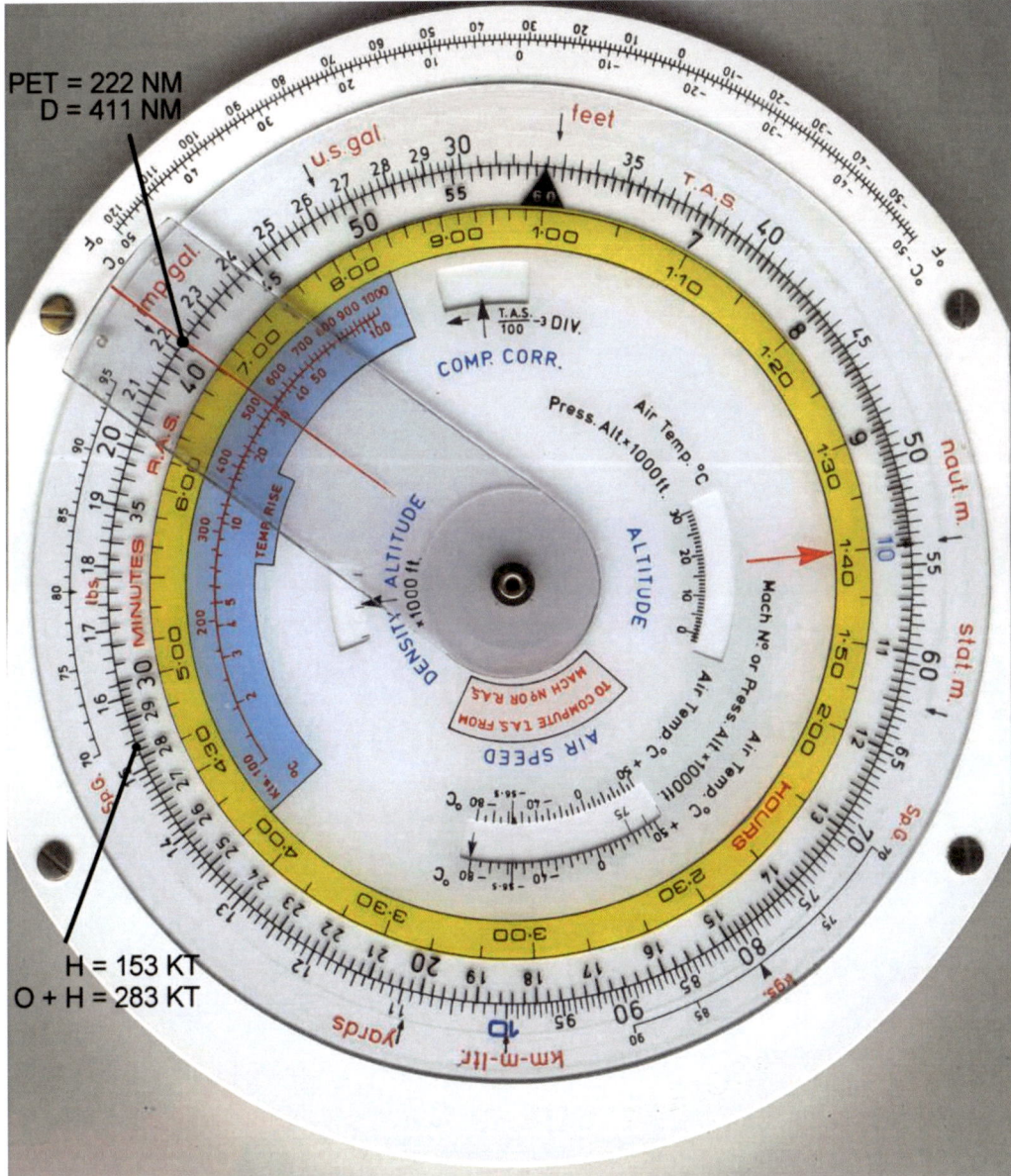

Figure 11.3 PET determination using CRP-5

CRANFIELD AVIATION TRAINING SCHOOL LTD. PART-FCL ATO N° 276
CATS INNOVATION CENTRE, LUTON, Bedfordshire LU2 8DL U.K.

www.catsaviation.com

11-6

Flight Planning & Monitoring

11.3.2 PSR

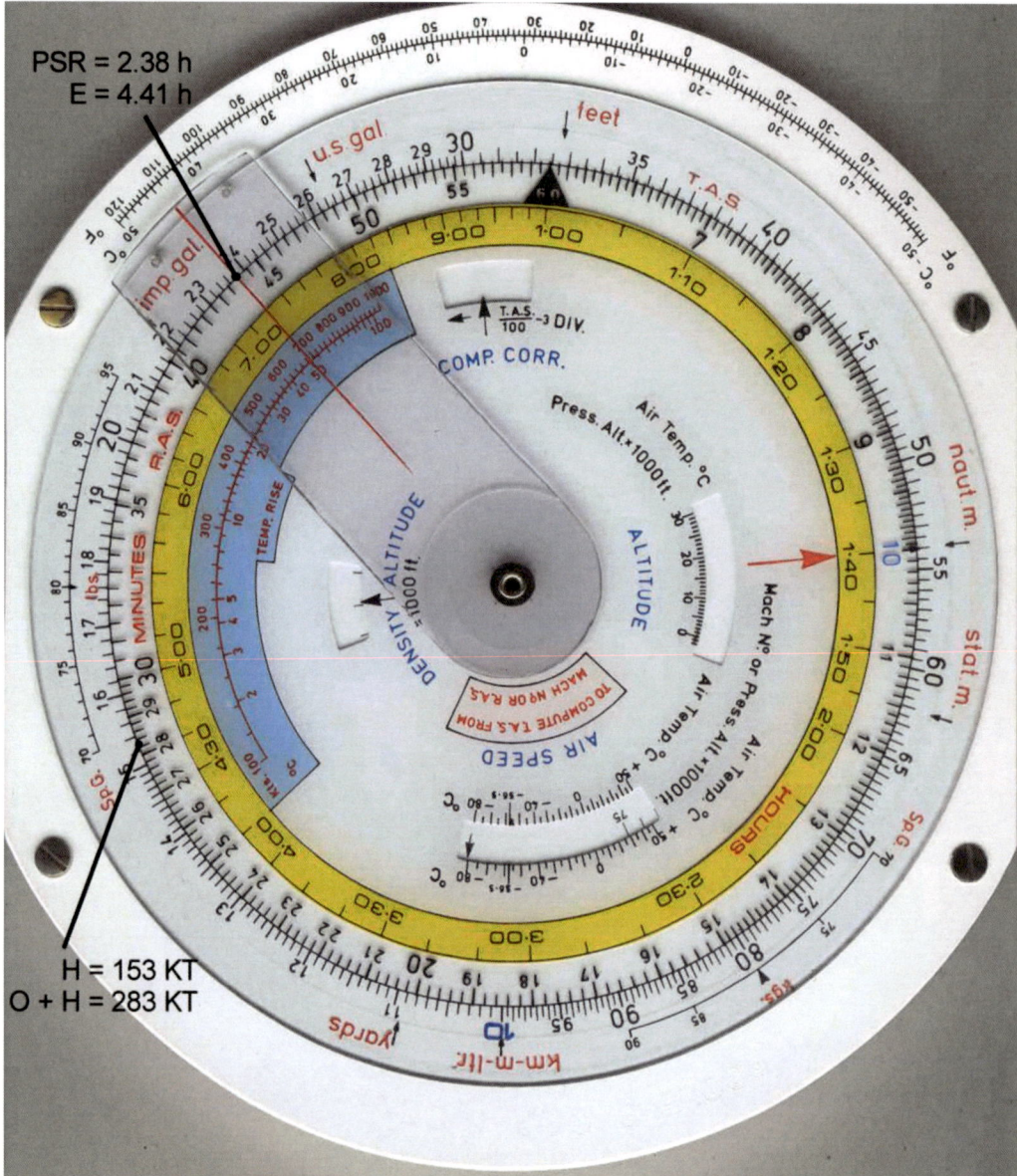

Figure 11.4 PSR determination using CRP-5

11.4 Multi-Leg PET's and PSR's

As we rarely fly direct to point B from point A, we need to evaluate PET's and PSR's along multiple legs.

In our flight from KUJACK to LA GRANDE RIVIERE, if we were to continue overhead and then turn south on to MATAGAMI NDB on airway J567, we can take a look at how it works.

First, lets list the details:

	Distance	Groundspeed out[1]	Groundspeed home[2]
YVP to YGL	411	152	153
YGL to NM	234	189	122

[1] = TAS 184 KT, [2] = Single-engine TAS 113 KT

	Time out	Time home
YVP to YGL	162mins	161mins
YGL to NM	74mins	115mins

Multi-leg PET

As we are considering times, we can see that it takes 6 minutes longer to fly back than to fly out. No surprise as we have considered returning with one engine shut down. But as we have seen, this is the same as the effect of a tailwind and using our gross error check, the PET should be prior to the half waypoint along track.

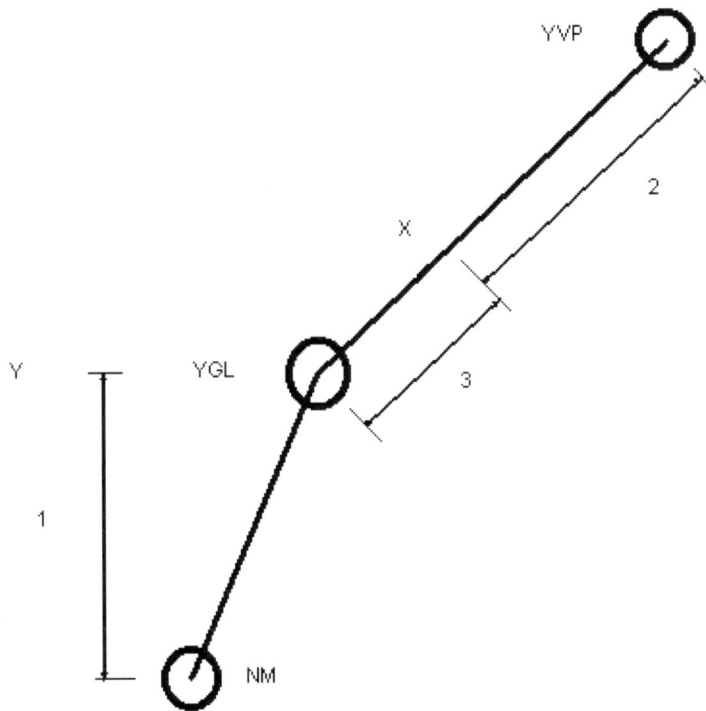

Figure 11.5

Firstly, we have to equalise the ends of the track to determine in what area the PET lies.

1. YGL to NM: 234 NM at 189 KT = 74 min
2. 74 min at 153 KT = 189 NM
3. 411 NM – 189 NM = 222 NM

Now, points X and Y are equal in TIME from YVP and NM respectively, leaving a 222 NM stretch of track along which our PET must lie. We can now apply our formula, treating this 222 NM track on it's own merits:

$$\frac{222 \times 153}{152 + 153} = \frac{33966}{305} = 111.36 \text{ NM}$$

So, distance and time to PET are:

216 + 111.36 = 327.36 NM
327.36 at 152 KT = 129 min (2 h 9 min)

CRANFIELD AVIATION TRAINING SCHOOL LTD. PART-FCL ATO N° 276
CATS INNOVATION CENTRE, LUTON, Bedfordshire LU2 8DL U.K.

www.catsaviation.com

11-8

Flight Planning & Monitoring

Total track distance YVP to NM:

411 + 234 = 645 $\frac{645}{2}$ = 322.5 NM

As you can see, the PET does lie in the first half of the Track.

11.4.1   Multi-leg PSR

Again, we try to pin down where along our route the PSR may lie. You may recall our endurance was 4 h 25 min, so what we do now is see how our endurance relates to the actual time it would take to fly out and back.

Some of this work we have already done:

YVP to YGL = 162mins
YGL to YVP = 161mins
                323mins   (5 h 23 min)

The PSR lies along the first leg, but if we were to plan on long range with reserves (45% power) using CAP 697, our endurance becomes 6 h 14 min approximately.

Now, we deduct the first leg out and back calculation of 323 min from our endurance of 374 min, giving 51 min (0.85 h)

Then we apply this to the leg YGL to NM as our new endurance figure within the PSR formula:

$\frac{0.85 \times 122}{189 + 122}$ = $\frac{103.7}{311}$ = 0.333440514 h (20min)

20mins at 189 KT = 63 NM beyond YGL

Our PSR therefore lies a total track distance of:

411 + 63 = 474 NM

And a time of:

162 + 20 = 182mins (3 h 2 min) from YVP.

11.5 The 'howgozit'

The howgozit is a graphical presentation of in-flight fuel usage

CAP 697 Figure 4.7.3 has been used in Figure 7.5 to derive a required fuel amount for a 1000 NM diversion, 1 engine inoperative, at 26000 ft, giving 4700 kg in a 25 KT tailwind.

It is assumed that the required reserve on return to P is 2 000 kg, thus at 1 000 NM out, required fuel is 2 000 + 4 700 = 6 700 kg.

2 000 kg at P and 6 700 kg 1 000 NM out allow a return fuel line to be added to the graph. The outbound fuel predictions run left to right, the return right to left. If the return line is extended it cuts the outbound line at 1 267 NM. This identifies the PSR at take off.

CRANFIELD AVIATION TRAINING SCHOOL LTD. PART-FCL ATO N° 276
CATS INNOVATION CENTRE, LUTON, Bedfordshire LU2 8DL U.K.   www.catsaviation.com

11-9   Flight Planning & Monitoring

It may be revised in flight thus:

At Q, usable fuel remaining in tanks is 12 500 kg and distance covered is 345 NM, plotted on the graph.

At R, usable fuel remaining in tanks is 9 500 kg and distance covered is 735 NM, also plotted on the graph.

If these two plots are connected and produced as a tendency, the intersection between this tendency and the return line is the revised position of the PSR at 1067 NM. This may be pessimistic since the tendency line has taken no account of the anticipated improvement in fuel economy after R.

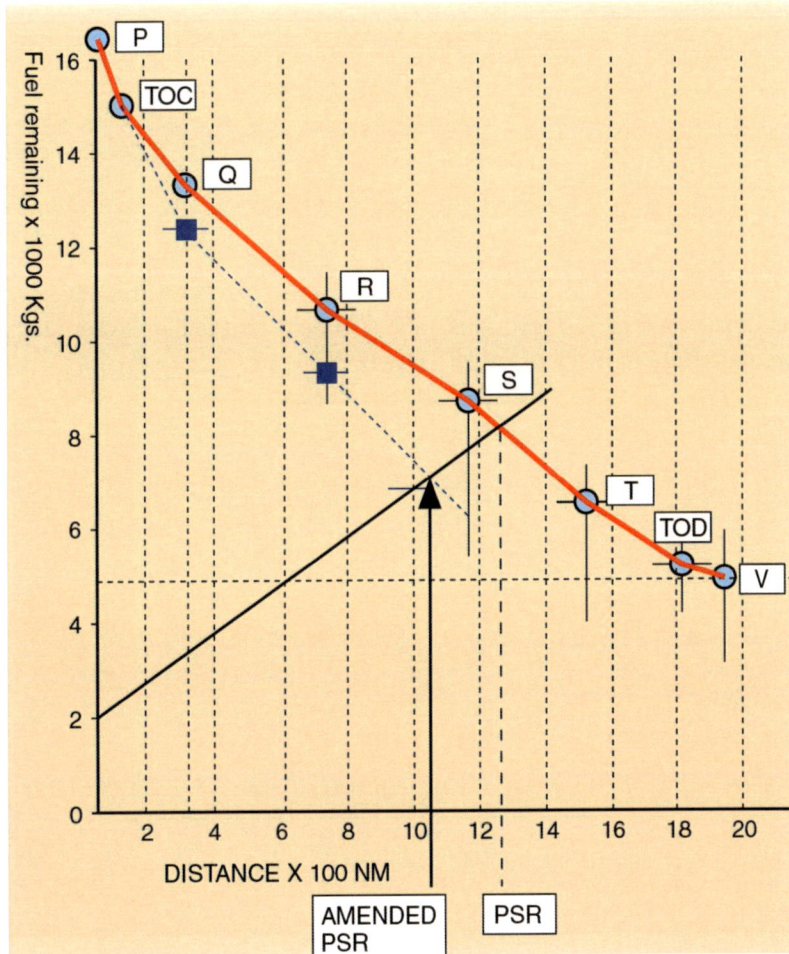

Figure 11.6 A howgozit showing 16 350 kg take off fuel and 4 800 kg fuel at landing

CRANFIELD AVIATION TRAINING SCHOOL LTD. PART-FCL ATO N° 276
CATS INNOVATION CENTRE, LUTON, Bedfordshire LU2 8DL U.K.

www.catsaviation.com

11-10

Flight Planning & Monitoring

Self Assessment Test 11

1   The correct formula to find distance to Point of Equal Time is:
A)   PET = Dist x GShome / (GSout + GShome)
B)   PET = (Dist / 2) x GSout / (GSout + GShome)
C)   PET = (Dist / 2) + GShome / (GSout + GShome)
D)   PET = Dist x GSout / (GSout + GShome)

2   Given:
    Distance A to B   2050 NM
    Mean groundspeed 'on'   440 KT
    Mean groundspeed 'back'   540 KT
    The distance to the point of equal time (PET) between A and B is:
A)   920 NM
B)   1025 NM
C)   1130 NM
D)   1153 NM

3   If CAS is 190 kts, Altitude 9000 ft. Temp. ISA - 10°C, True Course (TC) 350°, W/V 320/40, distance from departure to destination is 350 NM, endurance 3 hours and actual time of departure is 1105 UTC. The distance from departure to Point of Equal Time (PET) is :
A)   147 NM
B)   167 NM
C)   183 NM
D)   203 NM

4   Given :
    Course A to B 088° (T)
    distance 1250 NM
    Mean TAS 330 kt
    Mean W/V 340°/ 60 KT
    The time from A to the PET between A and B is:
A)   2 h 02 min
B)   1 h 39 min
C)   1 h 54 min
D)   1 h 42 min

5   Find the distance from waypoint 3 (WP 3) to the critical point.
    Given: distance from WP 3 to WP 4 = 750 NM, TAS out 430 kt, TAS return 425 kt, Tailwind component out 30 kt, head wind component return 40 kt
A)   342 NM
B)   375 NM
C)   403 NM
D)   408 NM

6   If CAS is 190 kts, Altitude 9000 ft. Temp. ISA - 10°C, True Course (TC) 350°, W/V 320/40, distance from departure to destination is 350 NM, endurance 3 hours, and actual time of departure is 1105 UTC. The Point of Equal Time (PET) is reached at :
A)   1203 UTC
B)   1213 UTC
C)   1221 UTC
D)   1233 UTC

7   What is the formula for Point of Safe Return (PSR)

A)   PSR = $\dfrac{\text{Dist} \times O \times H}{O + H}$

B)   PSR = $\dfrac{\text{Endurance} \times O \times H}{O + H}$

C)   PSR = $\dfrac{\text{Endurance} + O + H}{O + H}$

D)   PSR = endurance x O + H

8   Find the distance to the POINT OF SAFE RETURN (PSR).
    Given: maximum useable fuel 15000 kg, minimum reserve fuel 3500 kg, Outbound: TAS 425 kt, head wind component 30 kt, fuel flow 2150 kg/h, Return: TAS 430 kt, tailwind component 20 kt, fuel flow 2150 kg/h

A)   1463 NM
B)   1125 NM
C)   1143 NM
D)   1491 NM

9   Find the time to the Point of Safe Return (PSR).
    Given: Maximum useable fuel 15000 kg, Minimum reserve fuel 3500 kg, TAS out 425 kt, Head wind component out 30 kt, TAS return 430 kt, Tailwind component return 20 kt,
    Average fuel flow 2150 kg/h

A)   2 h 59 min
B)   2 h 43 min
C)   2 h 51 min
D)   3 h 43 min

10 Given :

Distance A to B	3060 NM
Mean groundspeed 'out'	440 KT
Mean groundspeed 'back'	540 KT
Safe Endurance	10 h

    The time to the Point of Safe Return (PSR) is:

A)   5 h 20 min
B)   5 h 30 min
C)   5 h 45 min
D)   3 h 55 min

CRANFIELD AVIATION TRAINING SCHOOL LTD. PART-FCL ATO N° 276
CATS INNOVATION CENTRE, LUTON, Bedfordshire LU2 8DL U.K.   www.catsaviation.com

11-12   Flight Planning & Monitoring

Self Assessment Test 11 Answers

1	A
2	C
3	D
4	D
5	A
6	B
7	B
8	B
9	C
10	B

CRANFIELD AVIATION TRAINING SCHOOL LTD. PART-FCL ATO N° 276
CATS INNOVATION CENTRE, LUTON, Bedfordshire LU2 8DL U.K.

www.catsaviation.com

11-13

Flight Planning & Monitoring

CHAPTER 12
Chart Legends

12.1 Appendix 2 to Annex 4 to the Convention on International Civil Aviation

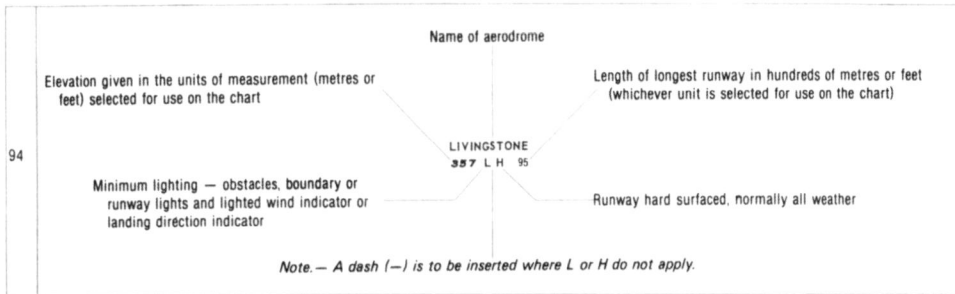

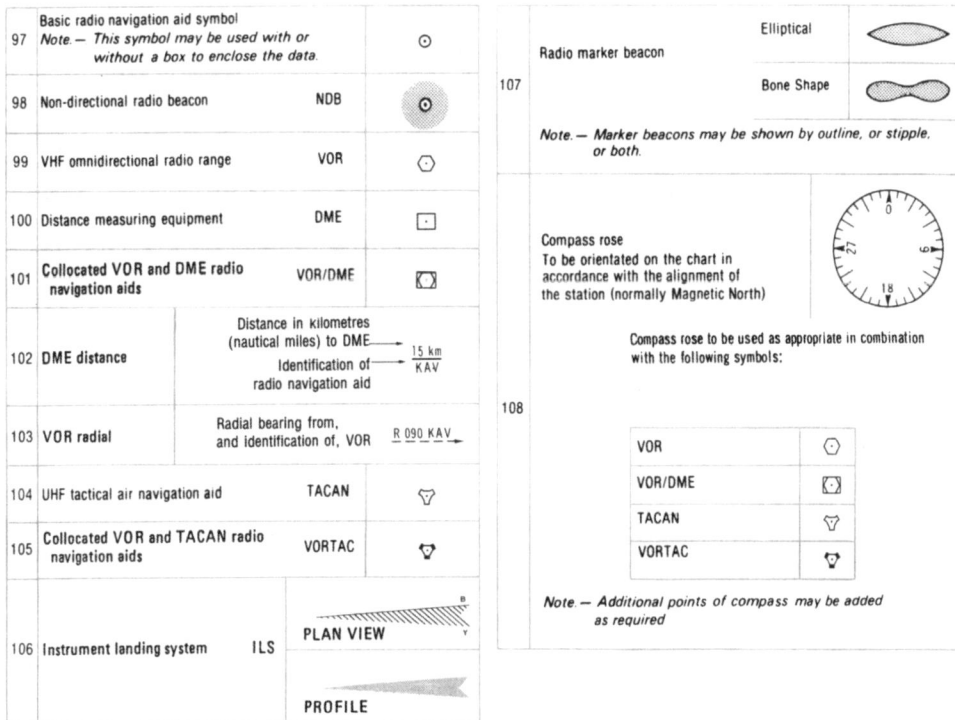

Figure 12.1

ICAO Chart Symbols

AIR TRAFFIC SERVICES

109	Flight information region	FIR	
110	Aerodrome traffic zone	ATZ	
111	Control area CTA Airway AWY Controlled route	Alternative	
112	Uncontrolled route		
113	Advisory airspace	ADA	
114	Control zone	CTR	
115	Advisory route	ADR Alternative	

116	Scale-break (on ATS route)	Alternative	
117	Reporting point	REP On request	▲ △
118	Change-over point COP To be superimposed on the appropriate route symbol at right angles to the route.		26 36
119	ATS/MET reporting point	MRP Compulsory On request	◪ ◪
120	Way-point WPT	Flyover WPT (also used for start point and end point of a controlled turn) Fly-by WPT	◆ ◇

AIRSPACE RESTRICTIONS

121	Restricted airspace (prohibited, restricted or danger area)		Common boundary of two areas	
	Note.— The angle and density of rulings may be varied according to scale and the size, shape and orientation of the area.			

122	International boundary closed to passage of aircraft except through air corridor	

OBSTACLES

123	Obstacle	⋀	127	Exceptionally high obstacle (optional symbol)	
124	Lighted obstacle		128	Exceptionally high obstacle — lighted (optional symbol)	
125	Group obstacles	⋀⋀		Note.— For obstacles having a height of the order of 300 m (1 000 ft) above terrain.	
126	Lighted group obstacles		129	Elevation of top (italics) 52 (15) Height above specified datum (upright type in parentheses)	

MISCELLANEOUS

130	Prominent transmission line		131	Isogonic line or isogonal	— 3°E —	132	Ocean station vessel (normal position)

VISUAL AIDS

133	Marine light		F ●	Note 1.— Marine alternating lights are red and white unless otherwise indicated. Marine lights are white unless colours are stated.			
	Note 2.— Characteristics are to be indicated as follows	Alt B F	Alternating Blue Fixed	Fl G Gp Flashing Green Group	Occ R SEC Occulting Red Sector	sec (U) W	Second Unwatched White

134	Aeronautical ground light	☆	135	Lightship	

Figure 12.2

CRANFIELD AVIATION TRAINING SCHOOL LTD. PART-FCL ATO N° 276
CATS INNOVATION CENTRE, LUTON, Bedfordshire LU2 8DL U.K.

www.catsaviation.com

12-2

Flight Planning & Monitoring

TOPOGRAPHY

1	Contours	*5000*	8	Gravel		12	Highest elevation on chart	*Alternative* 17456 / .17456
2	Approximate contours	*5500*	9	Levee or esker		13	Spot elevation	.6397 .8975
3	Relief shown by hachures					14	Spot elevation (of doubtful accuracy)	.6370 ±
4	Bluff, cliff or escarpment		10	Unusual land features appropriately labelled	Many Small Volcanoes / Rock Outcrop	15	Coniferous trees	
5	Lava flow					16	Other trees	
6	Sand dunes			Active volcano		17	Palms	
7	Sand area		11	Mountain pass	)-(5395			

18	Areas not surveyed for contour information or relief data incomplete

Caution

HYDROGRAPHY

19	Shore line (reliable)					38	Reservoir	■ *Reservoir*
20	Shore line (unreliable)		30	Abandoned canal Note.— Dry canal having landmark value.	– – – –			*Alternative*
21	Tidal flats		31	Lakes (perennial)		39	Dry lake bed	
22	Coral reefs and ledges		32	Lakes (non-perennial)		40	Wash	*Alternative*
23	Large river (perennial)		33	Salt lake		41	Shoals	
24	Small river (perennial)		34	Salt pans (evaporator)		42	Glaciers and ice caps	
25	Rivers and streams (non-perennial)	*Alternative*	35	Swamp		43	Danger line (2 m or one fathom line)	
26	Rivers and streams (unsurveyed)		36	Rice field	*Alternative*	44	Charted isolated rock	+
27	Rapids					45	Rock awash	⊕
28	Falls		37	Spring, well or water hole	perennial ●	46	Unusual water features appropriately labelled	*Covered Reef*
29	Canal				intermittent ○			

Figure 12.3

CRANFIELD AVIATION TRAINING SCHOOL LTD. PART-FCL ATO N° 276
CATS CATS INNOVATION CENTRE, LUTON, Bedfordshire LU2 8DL U.K.
www.catsaviation.com
Flight Planning & Monitoring

12-3

CULTURE

BUILT-UP AREAS

47	City or large town	
48	Town	o
49	Village	o
50	Buildings	

RAILROADS

51	Railroad (single track)	
52	Railroad (two or more tracks)	
53	Railroad (under construction)	
54	Railroad bridge	
55	Railroad tunnel	
56	Railroad station	

HIGHWAYS AND ROADS

57	Dual highway	
58	Primary road	
59	Secondary road	
60	Trail	
61	Road bridge	
62	Road tunnel	

MISCELLANEOUS

63	Boundaries (international)	
64	Other boundaries	
65	Fence	x—x—x
66	Telegraph or telephone line (when a landmark)	—T—T—
67	Dam	
68	Ferry	

MISCELLANEOUS (Cont'd)

69	Pipeline	Pipeline
70	Oil or gas field	
71	Tank farms	
72	Coast guard station	
73	Lookout tower	
74	Mine	
75	Forest ranger station	
76	Race track or stadium	
77	Ruins	
78	Fort	
79	Church	
80	Mosque	
81	Pagoda	
82	Temple	

AERODROMES

83	Civil Land	
84	Civil Water	
85	Military Land	
86	Military Water	

87	Joint civil and military Land	
88	Joint civil and military Water	
89	Emergency aerodrome or aerodrome with no facilities	

90	Sheltered anchorage	
91	Aerodrome for use on charts on which aerodrome classification is not required e.g. Enroute Charts	
92	Heliport Note.- Aerodrome for the exclusive use of helicopters	

93	Note.— Where required by the function of the chart, the runway pattern of the aerodrome may be shown in lieu of the aerodrome symbol, for example:

Figure 12.4

CHAPTER 13

Meteorology for Flight Planning

AIRLINE TRANSPORT PILOTS LICENCE
(030 00 00 00 - FLIGHT PERFORMANCE AND PLANNING)
033 00 00 00 FLIGHT PLANNING AND FLIGHT MONITORING
033 01 00 00 FLIGHT PLANS FOR CROSS-COUNTRY FLIGHTS FOR VFR FLIGHTS
033 01 01 03 Obtaining wind velocity forecast for each leg
-Wind
-At aerodromes
-At cruising levels
-Visibility
-Clouds and cloudbase
-Meteorological hazards

033 04 00 00 IFR (AIRWAYS) FLIGHT PLANNING
033 04 01 00 Meteorological considerations
033 04 01 01 Analysis of existing patterns alongside possible routes
☐Analyse the weather chart, locate and name the different weather systems on the route such as warm and cold fronts, occluded fronts, depressions, high pressure areas, hurricanes, thunderstorms

033 04 01 02 Analysis of winds aloft along prospective routes
☐Analyse the wind/ temperature for the relevant flight level(s), derive the estimated winds and temperatures along the prospective route for each leg

033 04 01 03 Analysis of existing and forecast weather conditions at destination and possible alternates
☐Analyse the TAF's and METAR's and determine the weather at the departure aerodrome, the destination and the alternates considering the following elements:
☐Wind
☐Visibility
☐Runway visual range
☐Thunderstorms
☐Precipitation
☐Cloud base
☐Temperature

033 06 00 00 PRACTICAL COMPLETION OF A FLIGHT PLAN (navigation plan/ flight log)
033 06 01 00 Extraction of data
033 06 01 02 Extraction of meteorological data
☐Obtain and decode the following meteorological data
☐Wind at different and appropriate levels and position of the jetstream
☐The presence of thunderstorms
☐Cloud base and thickness of cloud layers
☐Precipitation
☐Temperatures at different levels
☐Icing conditions
☐Areas of CAT and other turbulence

CRANFIELD AVIATION TRAINING SCHOOL LTD. PART-FCL ATO N° 276
CATS CATS INNOVATION CENTRE, LUTON, Bedfordshire LU2 8DL U.K.   www.catsaviation.com

13-1   Flight Planning & Monitoring

13.1 Observations and Reports for Take-off and Landing

13.1.1 Observing and Reporting of Surface Wind

The mean direction and the mean speed of the surface wind are reported in METARs and TAFs using the following format: wind direction in degrees true / wind speed in KT. The instantaneous wind velocity given to pilots on take-off or landing is in degrees magnetic. Other codes used in the measurement of wind speed are:
VRB – wind direction variable
CALM – wind speed less than 1 KT
G – gusting

13.1.2 Observing and Reporting of Visibility

Horizontal visibility is measured or observed by reference to objects whose distance from the point of observation is known. Units for visibility are in m or km, for example 0400 means 400 m, 1200 means 1200 m and 8000 means 8000 m or 8 km. A reported visibility of 9999 means 10 km or more.
When the visibility is not the same in different directions and the visibility is more than 50% above the lowest visibility, the lowest visibility in that direction should be reported with a suffix indicating the direction. For example, 1200 S means 1200 m to the South.

13.1.3 Observing and Reporting of Runway Visual Range

Runway visual range is reported from points alongside the runway parallel to the runway centre line when the runway visual range is observed to be less than 1500 m. For example, RVR RWY 32 400M. RVR is normally recorded within 300 m of the threshold. If more than one site is utilised the terms TDZ for touchdown zone, MID for midpoint and END for stop-end are used.

13.1.4 Observing and Reporting of Present Weather

Present weather phenomena are reported in terms of type and characteristics and qualified with respect to intensity and proximity to the aerodrome as follows:

Precipitation	
Drizzle	DZ
Rain	RA
Snow	SN
Snow Grains	SG
Ice Pellets	PL
Ice Crystals	IC
Hail	GR
Small Hail / Snow Pellets	GS

Obscuration	
Fog	FG
Mist	BR
Sand	SA
Dust	DU
Haze	HZ
Smoke	FU
Volcanic Ash	VA
Dust / Sand whirls (dust devils)	PO
Squall	SQ
Funnel Cloud (tornado or water spout)	FC
Duststorm	DS
Sandstorm	SS

Characteristics	
Thunderstorm	TS
Shower	SH
Freezing	FZ
Blowing	BL
Low Drifting	DR

Intensity		
Light	FBL	-
Moderate	MOD	(no indication)
Heavy	HVY	+

Shallow	MI
Patches	BC
Partial	PR
Vicinity	VC

13.1.5 Observing and Reporting of Cloud

Cloud amount, type and height of base are estimated to describe the general cloud distribution.

13.1.5.1 Cloud Amount

Cloud amount is described using a system based on oktas representing eighths of the sky covered:

		Eighths of sky covered
OVC	Overcast	8
BKN	Broken	5-7
SCT	Scattered	3-4
FEW	Few	1-2
SKC	Sky clear	0

When the sky is obscured, vertical visibility is reported if measurements are available in the form of VV followed by the units used (usually feet).

13.1.5.2 Type of Cloud

Type of cloud is only identified for cumulonimbus (CB) and towering cumulus (TCU).

13.1.5.3 Height of Cloud Base

Height of the base of cloud is reported in steps of 100' up to 10000' and in steps of 1000' above 10000'. For example, 004 means 400' and 040 means 4000' above aerodrome level.

13.1.6 Observing and reporting of air temperature and dew-point temperature

The air temperature and the dew-point temperature are reported to the nearest whole degree Celsius. Observed values involving 0.5 °C are rounded up to the next higher degree Celsius, for example, 2.5 °C would be rounded up to +3 °C and -2.5 °C should be rounded up to -2 °C. For a temperature below 0 °C the value should be preceded by M.

13.1.7 Observing and reporting of pressure values

The reference level for QFE is aerodrome elevation. The reference level for QNH is mean sea level. Values are rounded down to the nearest whole hectoPascal. For example, 995.6 hPa is reported as QNH 995.

13.1.8 Observing and reporting of supplementary information

Observations made at aerodromes should include all available supplementary information concerning meteorological conditions, particularly those in the approach and climb-out areas. This information is often abbreviated into plain language for example wind shear in the approach could be abbreviated to SURFACE WIND 320 / 10 KT AT 200' 360 / 25 KT IN APCH. Information on recent weather is reported with the prefix RE, for example, REFZRA – freezing rain occurred as recent weather in the last hour.

CRANFIELD AVIATION TRAINING SCHOOL LTD. PART-FCL ATO N° 276

CATS CATS INNOVATION CENTRE, LUTON, Bedfordshire LU2 8DL U.K.

www.catsaviation.com

13-3

Flight Planning & Monitoring

13.1.9   CAVOK

When the following conditions occur simultaneously at the time of observation the term CAVOK is used:

- Visibility 10 km or more
- No cloud below 5000' or minimum sector altitude whichever is higher
- No CB
- No significant weather

13.2   METARs

A prescribed format exists for the METAR as follows:

Report Identification
Location Indicator
Time of Observation
Surface Wind Velocity
Visibility
Runway Visual Range (if applicable)
Present Weather
Cloud Amount, Type and Base
Air temperature and Dew-point temperature
QNH
Supplementary Information

13.2.1   METAR Examples

Example:

SA1520 34010KT 8000 SKC 22/05 QI025 =

Decode: Surface Actual issued at 1520Z, wind direction 340, wind speed 10 KT, visibility 8000 m, sky clear, temperature 22 dew point 5, QNH 1025, end of message

Example:

EGKB 030950Z 22018G29KT 200V260 9999 SCT008 SCT020 12/10 Q1020 =

Decode: Biggin Hill, Surface Actual issued on the 3rd day of the month at 0950Z, wind direction 220 but varying between 200 and 260, wind speed 18 KT gusting up to 29 KT, visibility greater than 10 km, scattered cloud at 800', scattered cloud at 2000', temperature 12 dew point 10, QNH 1020, end of message

Example:

EGVN 101050Z 22015KT 9999 BKN012 14/11 Q1016 TEMPO 7000 –RA SCT006 =

Decode: Brize Norton, Surface Actual issued on the 10th day of the month at 1050Z, wind direction 220, wind speed 15 KT, visibility greater than 10 km, broken cloud at 1200', temperature 14 dew point 11, QNH 1016, temporary changes lasting less than 1 h (or less than half the duration of the message) of visibility decreasing to 7000 m with light rain and scattered cloud at 600', end of message

13.3   *TAFS*

Terminal Aerodrome Forecasts follow the same coded format as METARs. The duration of TAFs is 9 h, 18 h or 24 h.

13.3.1   *BECMG*

The change indicator BECMG and the associated time group are used to describe changes in the meteorological conditions at an unspecified time during the time period.

13.3.2   *TEMPO*

The change indicator TEMPO and the associated time group are used to describe expected frequent or infrequent temporary fluctuations in meteorological conditions which last for a period of less than 1 h in each instance and, in aggregate, cover less than one half of the forecast period during which the changes are expected to occur.

13.3.3   *PROB*

The probability of occurrence of an alternative value of a forecast element is indicated by use of PROB followed by the probability in tens of percent and the time period over which the alternative value is expected to occur. A probability of less than 30% is not indicated. A probability of 50% or more for aviation purposes is not considered a probability and instead should be indicated by the use of change indicators BECMG or TEMPO or by sub-division of the validity period using the abbreviation FM.

13.3.4   *NOSIG*

When no change is expected to occur the term NOSIG is used.

13.3.5   *TAF EXAMPLE*

Example:

EGKB 221212Z 221322 31014KT 9999 SCT030 TEMPO 1319 31015G25 5000 SHRA BKN025CB PROB40 TEMPO 1319 31020G35KT 2500 +TSRAGR BKN014CB =

Decode: Biggin Hill, 9 h Terminal Aerodrome Forecast issued on the 22nd day of the month at 1212Z, valid for the 9 h period from 1300Z to 2200Z, wind direction 310, wind speed 14 KT, visibility greater than 10 km, scattered cloud at 3000', temporary changes lasting less than 1 h (or less than half the duration of the message) between 1300Z and 1900Z of wind direction 310, wind speed 15 KT gusting up to 25 KT, visibility 5000 m in moderate showers of rain, cloud broken at 2500', cumulonimbus, probability of 40% of temporary changes lasting less than 1 h (or less than half the duration of the message) between 1300Z and 1900Z of wind direction of 310, wind speed 20 KT gusting up to 35 KT, visibility 2500 m with heavy showers of rain and hail, cloud broken at 1400', cumulonimbus =

13.4   *Upper wind and temperature charts for standard isobaric surfaces*

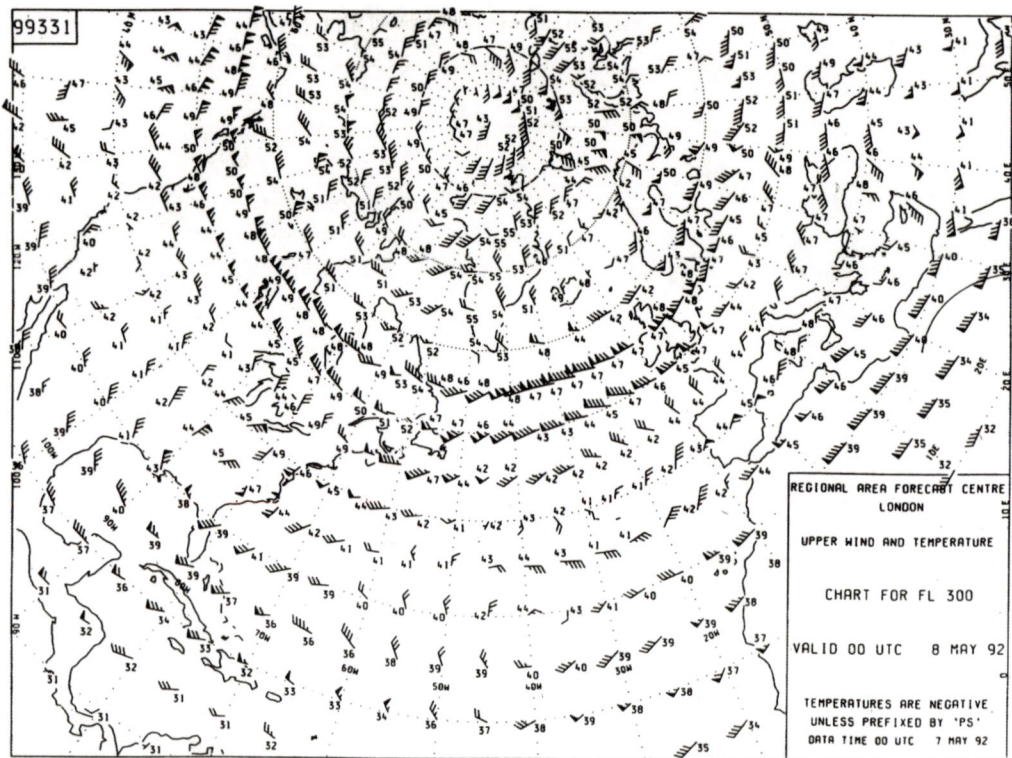

Figure 13.1   Upper Wind and Temperature Chart FL300 North Atlantic Region

CRANFIELD AVIATION TRAINING SCHOOL LTD. PART-FCL ATO N° 276
CATS INNOVATION CENTRE, LUTON, Bedfordshire LU2 8DL U.K.

www.catsaviation.com

13-6

Flight Planning & Monitoring

13.5   *Significant Weather Charts*

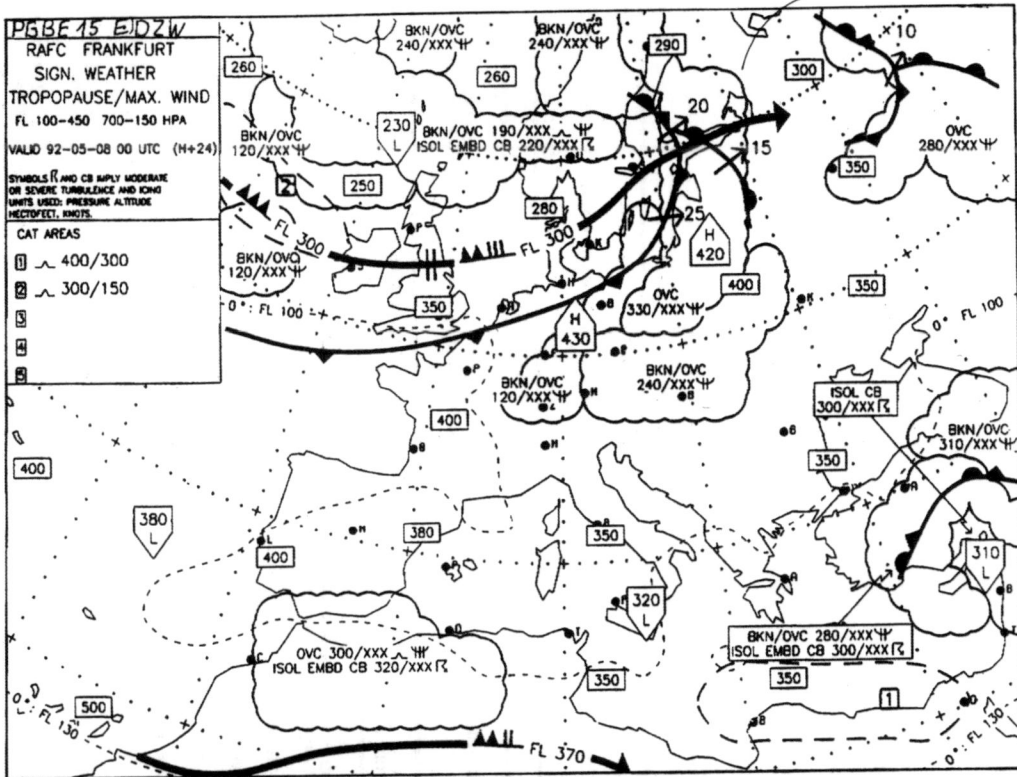

Figure 13.1   Significant Weather Chart

13.5.1   *Symbols for Significant Weather*

R	Thunderstorms	,	Drizzle
6	Tropical cyclone	/// /// /// ///	Rain
⌄-⌄-⌄	Severe squall line*	★	Snow
⌐ᴧ	Moderate turbulence	▽	Shower
⌐ᴧ̂	Severe turbulence	┼	Widespread blowing snow
◯	Mountain waves	S	Severe sand or dust haze
Ѱ	Moderate aircraft icing	Ƨ	Widespread sandstorm or dust storm
Ѱ̶	Severe aircraft icing	∞	Widespread haze
≡	Widespread fog	꞊	Widespread mist
△	Hail	ᴧᴧ	Widespread smoke
⛰	Volcanic eruption**	∿	Freezing precipitation ***
		▮	Visible ash cloud

13.5.2   Fronts and Convergence Zones and Other Symbols used

Symbol	Meaning	Symbol	Meaning
▲▲	Cold front at the surface	▲▲◣ FL 270	Position, speed and level of max. wind
●●	Warm front at the surface	↙	Convergence line
▲●▲●	Occluded front at the surface	0°:100	Freezing level
▲▼▲▼	Quasi-stationary front at the surface		Intertropical convergence zone
H 460	Tropopause High	10	State of the sea
270 L	Tropopause Low	18	Sea-surface temperature
380	Tropopause Level		

FL 340

▲▲◣◣◣ FL 300

Wind arrows indicate the maximum wind in the jet and the flight level at which it occurs. Significant changes (speed of 20 knots or more, 3 000 ft (less if practicable) in flight level) are marked by the double bar. In the example, at the double bar the wind speed is 225 km/h – 120 kt.

The heavy line delineating the jet axis begins/ends at the points where a wind speed of 150 km/h – 80 kt is forecast.

13.5.3   Abbreviations used to describe clouds

3.1 Type

CI = Cirrus
CC = Cirrocumulus
CS = Cirrostratus
AC = Altocumulus

AS = Altostratus
NS = Nimbostratus
SC = Stratocumulus

ST = Stratus
CU = Cumulus
CB = Cumulonimbus

3.2 Amount

Clouds except CB
SKC = sky clear (0/8)
FEW = few (1/8 to 2/8)
SCT = scattered (3/8 to 4/8)
BKN = broken (5/8 to 7/8)
OVC = overcast (8/8)

CB only
ISOL = individual CBs (isolated)
OCNL = well-separated CBs (occasional)
FRQ = CBs with little or no separation (frequent)
EMBD = CBs embedded in layers of other clouds or concealed by haze (embedded)

3.3 Heights

Heights are indicated on SWH and SWM charts in flight levels (FL), top over base. When XXX is used, tops or bases are outside the layer of the atmosphere to which the chart applies.
In SWL charts:
i)   Heights are indicated as altitudes above mean sea level;
ii) The abbreviation SFC is used to indicate ground level.

13.5.4   Arrows and Feathers

4.3 Arrows and feathers

Arrows indicate direction. Number of pennants and/or feathers correspond to speed.
Example:

▲▲◣◣   270°/115 kt (equivalent to 213 km/h)
            Pennants correspond to 50 kt or 93 km/h
            Feathers correspond to 10 kt or 18 km/h
            Half-feathers correspond to 5 kt or 9 km/h

CRANFIELD AVIATION TRAINING SCHOOL LTD. PART-FCL ATO N° 276
CATS INNOVATION CENTRE, LUTON, Bedfordshire LU2 8DL U.K.

www.catsaviation.com

13-8

Flight Planning & Monitoring

Self Assessment Test 13

1   For the following TAF:

EGLL 072200 0624 19005KT 6000 SCT030 PROB30 TEMPO 0608 1500 BR BECMG 0912 22010KT 9999 BECMG 1619 BKN035 =

What minimum visibility (m) is forecast for 0600 UTC at LONDON LHR (EGLL)?

A)   1500
B)   2200
C)   6000
D)   10000

Self Assessment Test 13 Answers

1	A

CRANFIELD AVIATION TRAINING SCHOOL LTD. PART-FCL ATO N° 276
CATS INNOVATION CENTRE, LUTON, Bedfordshire LU2 8DL U.K.

www.catsaviation.com

13-10

Flight Planning & Monitoring